DBT Therapeutic Activity Ideas for Working with Teens

of related interest

DBT-Informed Art Therapy
Mindfulness, Cognitive Behavior Therapy, and the Creative Process
Susan M. Clark
ISBN 978 1 84905 733 2
eISBN 978 1 78450 103 7

The CBT Art Activity Book
100 illustrated handouts for creative therapeutic work
Jennifer Guest
ISBN 978 1 84905 665 6
eISBN 978 1 78450 168 6

A Sad and Sorry State of Disorder
A Journey into Borderline Personality Disorder (and out the other side)
Tracy Barker
ISBN 978 1 78592 331 9
eISBN 978 1 78450 650 6

The Big Book of EVEN MORE Therapeutic Activity Ideas for Children and Teens
Inspiring Arts-Based Activities and Character Education Curricula
Lindsey Joiner
ISBN 978 1 84905 749 3
eISBN 978 1 78450 196 9

The Art Activity Book for Psychotherapeutic Work
100 Illustrated CBT and Psychodynamic Handouts for Creative Therapeutic Work
Jennifer Guest
ISBN 978 1 78592 301 2
eISBN 978 1 78450 607 0

Teen Anxiety
A CBT and ACT Activity Resource Book for Helping Anxious Adolescents
Raychelle Cassada Lohmann
ISBN 978 1 84905 969 5
eISBN 978 0 85700 859 6

DBT Therapeutic Activity Ideas for Working with Teens

Skills and Exercises for Working with Clients with Borderline Personality Disorder, Depression, Anxiety, and Other Emotional Sensitivities

Carol Lozier

Jessica Kingsley *Publishers*
London and Philadelphia

First published in 2018
by Jessica Kingsley Publishers
73 Collier Street
London N1 9BE, UK
and
400 Market Street, Suite 400
Philadelphia, PA 19106, USA

www.jkp.com

Library of Congress Cataloging in Publication Data
A CIP catalog record for this book is available from the Library of Congress

British Library Cataloguing in Publication Data
A CIP catalogue record for this book is available from the British Library

ISBN 978 1 78592 785 0
eISBN 978 1 78450 718 3

Printed and bound in Great Britain

The accompanying PDF can be downloaded from
www.jkp.com/voucher using the code t5ZKXPq6

Acknowledgments

I would like to express my thanks and gratitude to many:

First, to God, my cornerstone.

To my first DBT teen girls group, you all are amazing and will move mountains!

Mom and Dad, thank you for your guidance, and unwavering love and support.

Rachel, Dylan, Aaron, Ashley, Sydney, and Trey, you all are a blessing. I love every second of every minute with you all!

Lynn and Ronnie, thanks for your support. And especially to Lynn, my sweet sister, I love our story! I am so grateful to call you one of my best friends.

Mark and Shelley, thanks for your ability to bring humor to any situation.

Cherie, thanks for our sisterhood. It means the world to me.

John, my best friend and partner in life. Thank you for your humor and patience and support during a long summer of writing. You're the bestest!

Contents

Introduction

Adolescent mental health is a common concern in our society. Just reflecting on the names Columbine and Sandy Hook bring clear memories of devastation, loss, and of adolescents who suffered with emotional instability. Given the vulnerability of adolescents in today's world, it is our responsibility to teach young people the skills that they are missing due to mental health issues, and to any level of trauma they have endured.

In my practice as a therapist, I have specialized in treating those with trauma and, in particular, those who are adopted and foster children and teens. Initially, in my career, I focused on learning therapeutic modalities to heal the deep wounds of past trauma and loss. As I witnessed my clients healing from past traumas, I saw a reduction in their triggers, but noticed that they still struggled with unhealthy life skills, including hurtful coping skills: alcohol, drugs, self-cutting, self-harm, inordinate time asleep, excessive time on video games; emotional overreactions such as hitting, swearing, slamming doors, and refusing to comply with adult requests; and difficulty in getting along with others, for example in making and maintaining long-term relationships.

I began to search for another type of therapy to teach my clients these life skills, and found Dialectical Behavior Therapy (DBT). In my quest to learn DBT, I pursued online training from Dr Marsha M. Linehan's site, Behavioral Tech, and have been participating in a biweekly consultation group. In learning DBT, I quickly concluded that full healing for my clients meant that there needed to be a marriage between healing past trauma and addressing current behavior deficits. The addition of DBT skills in my practice gives me hope and the belief that teens can have a healthy and joy-filled life, and they have to learn new skills to accomplish these goals.

The Adolescent

Adolescence, ages 13 through 19, is an exciting and trying time as teens transition from childhood to adulthood. In this stage, teens face the developmental tasks and issues of self-identity and independence.

In self-identity, teens are discovering their own values, beliefs, and occupational and personal goals. Teens are trying to find out who they are as young adults, and what is important to them. They are discovering new interests and hobbies, possible occupations in adulthood, a changing relationship with family, and social relationships and dating.

Adolescents are also becoming independent, and separating from the family in which they were raised; this may be a birth family, foster family, adoptive family, or even a facility. This is a challenging time as teens negotiate accepting and managing greater levels of responsibility. At times, the teens may push for more independence than they, or their family, are ready for them to have.

DBT Skills Trainers

DBT skills are taught by skill trainers and, often in a group, there is a leader and a co-leader. Skills trainers need to know and use DBT skills in their daily life; the required level of training differs according to the population they serve. If the adolescent has any mental health disorder, they will need to learn DBT from a mental health practitioner, such as a social worker, psychologist, marriage and family counselor, or psychiatric nurse. Teens without any history of current mental health disorder can learn skills from anyone who is trained and practicing DBT, such as a parent, teacher, youth pastor, or other family members.

Certainly, skills trainers need to know and use DBT in their daily life. In addition, it is most important for a trainer to have a respectful and caring interaction and attitude with the teen. Trainers need to create a validating and nurturing environment for them. Teens need to feel heard and understood; and to know that you, as the adult, are walking alongside them in their learning process.

Introducing DBT to Teens and Families

As with any new class or skill acquisition, teens and their families may initially be guarded to the idea. Therefore, introducing DBT to teens and families is crucial to gaining their compliance. Trainers can use the following statements as they dialogue with parents to express DBT's ability to improve a teen's life:

> DBT is a skills-based program where teens learn practical coping skills to improve their ability to focus their attention, manage feelings, deal with life stresses, and get along better with others. DBT has four groups of skills, and within each group there are numerous hands-on tools for teens to learn and use, creating a life in balance. DBT skills are a valuable toolkit for teens to have with them and use in any setting.

The Activity Book

The activity book does not go into vast detail on how to use DBT skills or manage a DBT skills group, rather it is meant to be a supplement to comprehensive DBT skills books or programs. The activity book offers fun and unique DBT skills handouts and worksheets for skills trainers to engage adolescents into a DBT practice.

Readers can gain more in-depth knowledge about DBT skills and DBT skills training at Behavioral Tech (for details, see the References), and in the following books: *DBT Skills Training Handouts and Worksheets* (Linehan, 2015a), *DBT Skills Training Manual* (Linehan, 2015b), *DBT Skills in Schools* (Mazza *et al.*, 2016), and *DBT Skills Manual for Adolescents* (Rathus and Miller, 2015).

All the handouts and worksheets in the activity book are based on DBT skills created by Marsha Linehan (2015a and 2015b), unless otherwise noted. A few handouts or worksheets are adapted from information from Dr James J. Mazza *et al.* (2016), and Dr Cathy Moonshine (2008).

The DBT skills handouts and worksheets are divided into four parts, following the four modules of DBT: Mindfulness, Distress Tolerance, Emotion Regulation, and Interpersonal Effectiveness. While the handouts and worksheets have been created for teens, they can be adapted or used with children and adults, too. Handouts and worksheets can be used individually or in group settings. They can be a stand-alone activity or incorporated into a traditional, weekly DBT skills group.

To begin with, each chapter will briefly describe the DBT skill. Typically, handouts will explain the skill while worksheets will individualize and offer practice in using the skill. Remember, for further details about each skill, refer to the skills books mentioned above and later again in the References.

Following the skill description, each chapter has directions on how to use the handout and worksheet; a completed example of the worksheet will precede the blank form. The blank worksheet will be given to your teen to fill out according to their individual ideas and understanding of the DBT skill. If the blank worksheet does not have enough space to write on, encourage the teen to use the back page of the worksheet to complete their answer. The handouts and worksheets can be photocopied and downloaded from www.jkp.com/voucher using the code t5ZKXPq6.

In the process of learning new information, everyone tends to have a mixture of learning styles: auditory, visual, and kinesthetic (hands-on learning). Many of your teens will have a primary learning style, and some may have a secondary style as well. I have incorporated images on the handouts and worksheets in order to further reach visual learners. This includes creative fonts, the typical DBT acronyms, and fun images. Along with the visual help, I encourage you to find ways to add auditory support through discussing the worksheets, and suggesting that teens read the worksheets silently to themselves or aloud within the group. Where possible, incorporate kinesthetic learning through role plays or body movement.

I have noticed my own personal challenge in recalling which of the skills fall into the different modules of: mindfulness, distress tolerance, emotion regulation, and interpersonal effectiveness. To hasten the teens' learning, I have included a circled initial of each skill group on the relevant handouts and worksheets, for example:

mindfulness = mi

distress tolerance = dt

emotion regulation = er

interpersonal effectiveness = ie

I am excited for your teen's journey into a DBT lifestyle! As they delve into learning and practicing the skills, they will find it immensely helpful in daily life. The more the teens use the skills, the more successful they will become and embrace "a life worth living!"

Section 1

What is DBT?

1. What is Dialectical Behavior Therapy (DBT)?

In the 1990s, Marsha Linehan created Dialectical Behavior Therapy (DBT). Although DBT was originally created for adults, it has been modified to be used for teens since around 2011. DBT was originally created to treat individuals with borderline personality disorder and chronic suicidal ideation. Currently, it is shown to be an effective way to treat a wide variety of psychological issues.

DBT is a highly researched group of practical tools to help teens manage their emotions and emotional crises, and to get along better with others. Teens learn DBT skills to replace their old, ineffective behaviors with new, effective ones.

DBT teaches skills to teens in individual and group settings, and in multifamily groups. The teen is assigned homework in order to practice the skills in their daily life at school, home, and in the community. Typically, teens are in a weekly skills-based group for six months to a year, and in individual skills training as well. In individual and group sessions, teens begin with a mindfulness exercise, review their homework, and then learn a new DBT skill.

DBT is composed of four groups of skills or modules: Mindfulness, Distress Tolerance, Emotion Regulation, and Interpersonal Effectiveness. Within each skill module, there are numerous hands-on tools for teens to learn and use, and to create a life in balance. It is extremely valuable for parents or another adult to learn and implement DBT skills alongside the teen so as to ensure their success in incorporating the skills into their daily life.

The four modules of DBT

1. *Mindfulness*: In DBT, mindfulness is a fundamental part of all skills. Mindfulness is the practice of being in the moment, without judgment towards ourselves and others, and maintaining an awareness of our thoughts, feelings, body sensations, and environment.

   Teens need to create a consistent, daily practice of mindfulness to improve their ability to focus and to increase feelings of happiness. Mindfulness is composed of two parts: WHAT and HOW skills. The WHAT skills include: observe, describe, and participate; and the HOW skills include: non-judgmentally, one-mindfully, and effectively.

2. *Distress Tolerance*: Distress tolerance skills teach teens to stay out of emotional crises ranging from out-of-control emotions and behavior (i.e., yelling, hitting, throwing things, swearing), to complete shutdown of emotions and behavior (i.e., refusing to talk, avoiding eye contact, curling up into a ball). The skills help teens get through difficult emotions, and through crisis situations that they have to deal with or accept as a reality.

   Distress tolerance is composed of crisis survival and reality acceptance skills. Crisis survival skills help the teens to problem-solve in the moment without impulsively reacting and making the situation worse. Reality acceptance skills focus on the teen accepting a situation as it is without trying to fight it.

3. *Emotion Regulation*: In emotion regulation skills, teens learn to manage unwanted emotions. In this module, emotion regulation skills teach your teen to know his or her emotions: how to recognize and identify feelings, and how to deal with them, staying in charge of emotions even when the teen may be vulnerable.

   They also explore and get to know emotions by asking questions such as, "What are my emotions?" and "How do I experience my emotions: how do they make me feel in my body, my voice, and my facial expressions?" Additionally, the skills in this module teach teens to handle negative emotions and to build on positive ones.

4. *Interpersonal Effectiveness*: Teens have to learn to handle relationships in an effective manner. For the teen, relationships may be with parents, foster family, siblings, teachers, coaches, peers, neighbors, and also themselves. DBT skills teach teens to maintain relationships, get their needs met in a healthy way, and maintain self-respect.

In addition, teens will learn to repair wrongdoing or mistakes with others; to self-monitor and to use true, helpful, inspiring, necessary, and kind words with others; give and accept emotional support from others; and, finally, they will learn to recognize behaviors that potentially end relationships.

~ Handout Directions ~

The "4 Modules" handout assists the skills trainer in explaining the four modules of DBT. Use the above information as well as other sources to explain mindfulness, distress tolerance, emotion regulation, and interpersonal effectiveness. There is additional space at the bottom of each list to include additional points that you would like your teen to remember.

What is DBT?

4 Modules

MINDFULNESS:

- focus attention in the moment
- be non-judgmental
- be fully aware of your emotions and senses.

EMOTION REGULATION:

- understand your emotions
- manage your emotions
- tolerating problematic emotions.

DISTRESS TOLERANCE:

- get through hard times and manage frustrations
- actively problem-solving
- fully accepting reality... even if you don't agree with it.

INTERPERSONAL EFFECTIVENESS:

- getting your needs met in relationships
- respecting yourself and others
- repairing relationships
- communicating effectively.

Adapted from Linehan, *DBT Skills Training Manual* (2015b)

~ Worksheet Directions ~

For this worksheet, there are two options for the skills trainer to choose from. You can either allow the teen to pick the worksheet of their choosing or you can use both at different times to emphasize the importance of the four modules of DBT.

Provide a worksheet to each teen. Review the four modules of DBT or let the teens take turns reviewing the modules with one another. In the circle or under each banner, teens will write their understanding of each module that has previously been described to them. This is a great opportunity to ensure that they understand the basic foundational information of the four modules of DBT.

What is DBT?

4 Modules

MINDFULNESS:

EMOTION REGULATION:

DISTRESS TOLERANCE:

INTERPERSONAL EFFECTIVENESS:

What is DBT?

4 Modules

MINDFULNESS IS...

Be in the moment, with awareness, without judgment

EMOTION REGULATION IS...

Identify feelings and stay in charge of them

DISTRESS TOLERANCE IS...

Get through hard emotions and crises

INTERPERSONAL EFFECTIVENESS IS...

Build and keep relationships, with self-respect

What is DBT?

4 Modules

MINDFULNESS IS...

EMOTION REGULATION IS...

DISTRESS TOLERANCE IS...

INTERPERSONAL EFFECTIVENESS IS...

2. Biosocial Theory

Linehan (2015b) based DBT on biosocial theory. She explains that emotionally sensitive children raised in an invalidating environment can later have difficulty regulating their emotions and/or controlling their behavior.

Following biosocial theory, some teens have a biological predisposition for emotional sensitivity. These teens tend to be emotionally reactive or sensitive, and have a hard time returning to a state of calm after a period of emotional dysregulation. Oftentimes, teens experience great relief when they learn of biosocial theory. It is comforting to understand that there is a biological base to their emotional sensitivity.

An invalidating environment reflects one where the emotions of the child are criticized or "invalidated" by his or her significant others causing the child to feel unheard or misunderstood, and that his or her emotions are weird, wrong, or bad. As an example, a child is scared and cries; the adult responds to the situation by mocking the child or by saying, "Toughen up! You're being ridiculous!"

~ *Worksheet Directions* ~

Provide a "Biosocial Theory" worksheet for each teen, and explain biosocial theory. Describe the concepts of "emotional sensitivity" and "invalidating environment" as described above and from other sources. Next, encourage the teens to write examples of their own emotional sensitivity and feelings of invalidation from within their own personal environments: home, school, church, or community. If the teens feel comfortable, they can share their answers with the group. (Remember, the first worksheet is a completed one and serves as an example for the teens.)

What is DBT?

Biosocial Theory

EMOTIONALLY SENSITIVE

+

INVALIDATING ENVIRONMENT

- Ignore
- Judge
- Deny

- Pick up others' emotions
- Fast reactions
- Hard time getting back to calm

My examples:

EMOTIONALLY SENSITIVE

- I get mad really fast.
- Sometimes, I get so mad, I can't calm down.

INVALIDATING ENVIRONMENT

- Mom will yell at me when I'm already upset.
- Dad ignores my feelings.
- My friends at school call me crazy.

What is DBT?

Biosocial Theory

EMOTIONALLY SENSITIVE
+
INVALIDATING ENVIRONMENT

- Pick up others' emotions
- Fast reactions
- Hard time getting back to calm

- Ignore
- Judge
- Deny

My examples:

EMOTIONALLY SENSITIVE

INVALIDATING ENVIRONMENT

3. The "D" in DBT

Teens can get stuck in their thinking. They may get caught up in thinking that they are "right" and others are "wrong," or that things are "unfair" and need to be "fair." They may also get entangled in how things "should" or "shouldn't" be. Teens may see the world in rigid, black-or-white thinking rather than in its reality… varying shades of gray.

The "D" in DBT stands for "dialectical." Dialectics is the concept of holding two opposite thoughts in balance and accepting that they can both be true. Even if it does not feel like it, there are always some shades of truth to opposing beliefs or to other people's points of view. Engaging in dialectical thinking helps adolescents to be more flexible with other people.

One foundational dialectic in DBT is acceptance and change. This belief states that teens need to accept themselves as they are while still admitting to their need for change and growth. Additional examples of dialectical thinking for a teen are:

"I can ask for help and become responsible and independent."

"I want to have fun and be free, and I want to follow the rules."

"I want to be a good student and I don't want to study."

Examples of dialectical thinking for a parent or caregiver are:

"My teen is doing the best he/she can, and he/she can try harder."

"I love my child and dislike his or her choices."

~ *Worksheet Directions* ~

Provide "The D in DBT" worksheet for each teen, and explain the idea of dialectical thinking from your sources. Following the explanation, ask the teens to show their understanding of dialectics through writing four dialectical statements of their own. These statements can reflect their own life or simply be dialectical statements that they have created. In this exercise, teens can work individually or in pairs. If they are willing, ask the teens to share their dialectical statements with the group.

What is DBT?

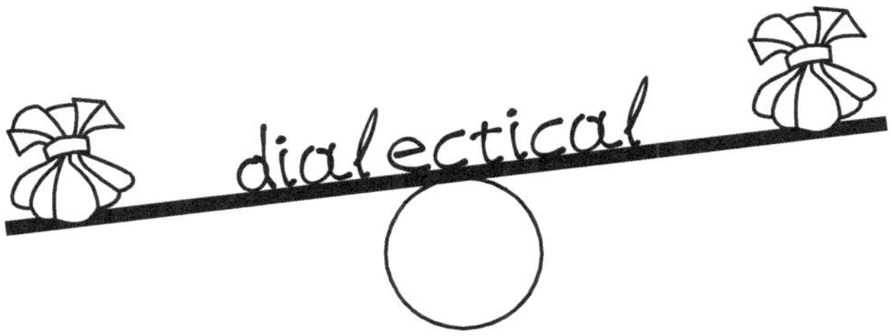

The "D" in DBT

Following are my examples of dialectical thinking:

1. I can ask for help and become independent.

2. I want my room to be clean and I don't want to hang up my clothes.

3. I want to lose some weight and I want to eat that bowl of ice cream.

4. I want to have fun and be free and I want to follow my parent's rules.

What is DBT?

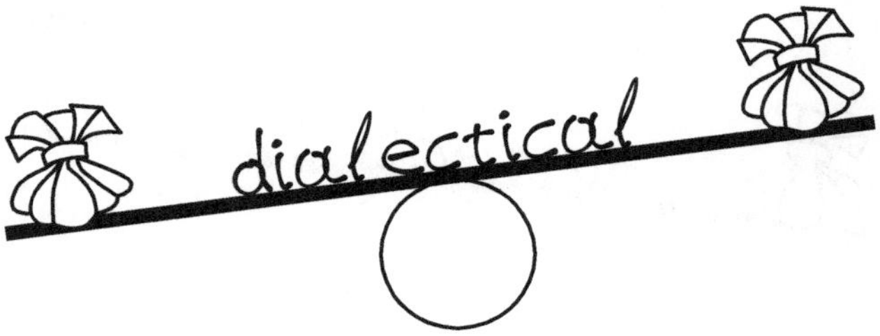

The "D" in DBT

Following are my examples of dialectical thinking:

1.

2.

3.

4.

4. DBT Acronyms

Both acronyms and abbreviations are formed from the initial letters of words; however, while acronyms form words from the initial letters, abbreviations do not. Acronyms are heavily relied upon in DBT, and as you browse through the worksheets, you will notice many of them. Commonly, they are used in DBT to help a teen learn and memorize DBT skills. DBT can be a very creative therapy, and if your teen does not like a particular acronym, allow them to change it to something more relevant, as long as they maintain the meaning of the skill.

~ Worksheet Directions ~

Provide an "Acronyms worksheet" for each teen. At the same time, give each of the teens the coordinating handout found in Section 1, Skill 7(b), called "Positive Personal Attributes." To make the task of creating an acronym a bit easier, they are welcome to use the "Positive Personal Attributes" handout for ideas of positive, uplifting adjectives to describe themselves.

After passing out the "Acronyms" worksheet, ask your teen to create an acronym from the letters in their name. Each word of the acronym should describe one of their positive personal characteristics. Instruct the teens to use only validating and encouraging words: we want to use every opportunity to build up their self-esteem!

Hint: See the two completed worksheets following this explanation as further example.

Acronyms

Create an acronym from your first name with validating, encouraging words.

A = adorable

a = agreeable

r = responsible

o = observant

n = nice

___ =

___ =

___ =

___ =

___ =

___ =

Acronyms

Create an acronym from your first name with validating, encouraging words.

R = rosy

A = adorable

C = cheery

H = humble

E = energetic

L = lovely

___ =

___ =

___ =

___ =

___ =

Acronyms

Create an acronym from your first name with validating, encouraging words.

___ =

___ =

___ =

___ =

___ =

___ =

___ =

___ =

___ =

___ =

___ =

5. DBT is a Lifestyle

Learning DBT skills takes time and practice. It is valuable for your teen to incorporate DBT into their daily life, much like someone recently diagnosed with a physical illness must learn and follow a new self-care plan.

As teens progress into adolescence, they go through the developmental stage of becoming autonomous from parents and other adults. As a result, learning DBT skills becomes entangled with this developmental task. Parents and clinicians must balance allowing the teen to decide that learning DBT skills are a priority, while gently encouraging them to incorporate skills into their lifestyle. Some of the ways in which to accomplish this balance include: teaming up with the teen rather than demanding that they learn the skills; validating and showing respect for their decision-making abilities; discussing the pros and cons of learning the skills; encouraging their independent thinking; and making sure not to criticize their beliefs even if you disagree with them.

The "DBT is a Way of Life to Learn and Practice" worksheet contains four statements/questions. Let's discuss each one further.

Discuss statement number one with the teens, "Reasons to make DBT part of my life," or in DBT language, "Building a life worth living." As the teens hear a peer's answer, it may positively influence them to participate more fully in learning DBT skills, or they may contemplate a point that they had not previously considered.

Question two is: "What are some of my thoughts and behaviors that might get in the way of a DBT life?" Discuss some examples and solutions with the teen or group. DBT refers to this as, "Therapy-Interfering Behaviors." Again, it is immensely helpful for teens to hear solutions and a desire to change from others.

The final two questions examine the teen's support group, and how they can elicit support from their family, friends, school, religious organization, and other trusted adults. Inspire the teens to ask for support from others, and encourage them to try new ways that they have not attempted before. As they hear suggestions for gaining support from others, it may spur them to try new ideas.

~ *Worksheet Directions* ~

Give the "DBT is a Way of Life to Learn and Practice" worksheet to each teen. Begin by asking the teens to name their favorite activities, e.g., sports, hobbies, academic subjects. Point out to them that their accomplishment came from practice or the repetition of those skills. Explain through comparison that DBT skills are also best understood and utilized when they are regularly practiced and become a way of life.

What is DBT?

DBT is a Way of Life to Learn and Practice

1. Reasons to make DBT part of my life:

- have a close, healthy friendship
- less depressed
- no fits
- have healthy relationships with my parents.

2. What are some of my thoughts and behaviors that might get in the way of a DBT life?

- missing DBT group
- "it's too hard"
- not doing my DBT homework.

3. Who are the people who can support me as I learn and practice DBT?

- Mom and Dad
- my sister
- my friend, Allie
- my youth pastor
- my counselor, Ms. Weiner.

4. What are some ways in which I'd like people to support me?

LIST

- Be patient with me.
- Validate me.

What is DBT?

DBT is a Way of Life to Learn and Practice

1. Reasons to make DBT part of my life:

2. What are some of my thoughts and behaviors that might get in the way of a DBT life?

3. Who are the people who can support me as I learn and practice DBT?

4. What are some ways in which I'd like people to support me?

LIST

6. Logs (Diary Cards)

Diary cards or logs are a handy way to encourage teens to practice and keep track of their DBT skill usage. They are also a means for the parent or clinician to see what the teen is practicing, and whether they understand and are using the skills. And, in line with teens' drive for independence, it is an easy way to find out what they are doing without getting into the power struggle of asking, "Did you practice?"

I have included several forms of diary cards, or logs, to allow teens to have more voice in their preference. There is a daily log and a weekly log. The logs will reflect the teen's practice of DBT skills for group or individual sessions, and may also include information regarding sleep habits, mood fluctuations, school and chore compliance, and self-care and hygiene.

~ Worksheet Directions ~

Allow your teen to choose a diary card or log that best fits their personality and daily life. They can choose a log that is more detailed or one that gives them the opportunity to write their own target behaviors. If they find that they do not like the log that they have chosen, they can simply try another one the following week.

Daily Log

DBT practice

MINDFULNESS

- observe, describe, participate
- non-judgmental
- one-mindful

DISTRESS TOLERANCE

- improve—I did encouragement
- TIP
- half-smile

EMOTION REGULATION

- ABC cope ahead with Mom
- Opposite Action

INTERPERSONAL EFFECTIVENESS

- Repairs—with Rachel
- GIVE

Habit tracker

	AM	PM
Brush/floss teeth	☒	☒
Shower	☒	○
Wash face	☒	☒
Fix my hair	☒	○
Face medicine	○	☒
________	○	○

Chores

- ☒ Make bed
- ☒ Take out trash
- ☐
- ☐
- ☐

I slept 7½ hours last night

Mood

	(1–10)
Sad	2
Happy	3
Angry	7
________	____

School

- ☒ Homework
- ☒ Study 2 hours
- ☐ Work on upcoming project
- ☐ Practice (music, dance)
- ☐

Physical care

- ○ 20–30 minutes of exercise
- ☒ 4 glasses of water
- ☒ Vitamins
- ☒ Medicines taken:
  - ○ AM
  - ☒ PM—Zoloft
- ☒ No drug/alcohol use
- ☒ No self-harm/picking

Daily Log

DBT practice

MINDFULNESS

-
-
-

DISTRESS TOLERANCE

-
-
-

EMOTION REGULATION

-
-

INTERPERSONAL EFFECTIVENESS

-
-

Habit tracker

	AM	PM
Brush/floss teeth	o	o
Shower	o	o
Wash face	o	o
________	o	o
________	o	o
________	o	o

Chores

- ☐
- ☐
- ☐
- ☐
- ☐

I slept ___ hours last night

Mood

	(1–10)
Sad	___
Happy	___
Angry	___
______	___

School

- ☐ Homework
- ☐ Study __ hours
- ☐ Work on upcoming project
- ☐ Practice (music, dance)
- ☐

Physical care

- 20–30 minutes of exercise
- __ glasses of water
- Vitamins
- Medicines taken:
  - AM
  - PM
- No drug/alcohol use
- No self-harm/picking

Weekly Log

Monday o o o o o o	Friday o o o o o o
Tuesday o o o o o o	Saturday o o o o o o
Wednesday o o o o o o	Sunday o o o o o o
Thursday o o o o o o	– NOTES –

7. Lists, Information, and Suggestions

This section presents a series of handouts that coordinate with worksheets found throughout the activity book. The handouts contain information, lists, and suggestions to help the teen further understand or put certain DBT skills into practice.

7(a) Accumulate positive pleasant activities practice

This list of pleasant activities coordinates with the emotion regulation skill, ABC, found in emotion regulation skills, Section 4, Skill 3. The handout offers a list of pleasant activities suggestions to complete the "Accumulate Positive Emotions" portion of the "ABC" worksheet in the same section. Again, "Accumulate Positive Emotions" is part of the ABC skill designed to help teens increase positive emotions and pleasurable experiences in life.

~ *Handout Directions* ~

Give the handout to your teen along with the worksheet "ABC" (Section 4, Skill 3). The teen can peruse this list to help generate a list of activities they enjoy to complete the "Accumulate Positives" portion of the ABC skill.

Once the teens have compiled their short- and long-term lists, they can share them aloud with one another. This is an opportunity for the teens to share and learn additional ideas from one another.

Accumulate Positives

Pleasant activities list

1. Play with a dog or cat.
2. Take a warm bath.
3. Take your dog for a walk.
4. Read an entertaining book.
5. Watch a funny movie.
6. Get a manicure or pedicure.
7. Get a hot stone massage.
8. Play your favorite sport or do your workout.
9. Pray.
10. Take pictures of animals or nature.
11. Make a fun craft project.
12. Listen to music.
13. Take a scenic drive.
14. Talk to a friend or mentor.
15. Go on a bike ride.
16. Write in a journal.
17. Sing to uplifting music.
18. Doodle.
19. Draw your favorite relaxing place.
20. Laugh out loud.
21. Drink warm hot chocolate.
22. Practice mindfulness.
23. Browse a home or clothes catalog.
24. Cook a healthy meal.
25. Watch your favorite sports team.

7(b) Positive personal attributes

This list of positive personal attributes coordinates with the worksheet "DBT Acronyms," found in Section 1, Skill 4. As a reminder, acronyms are a mnemonic commonly used in learning DBT skills.

~ *Handout Directions* ~

Provide this handout to your teen along with the coordinating "DBT Acronyms" worksheet, located in Section 1, Skill 4. This handout assists the teens in generating a list of positive personal attributes to create an acronym of their first name. As the acronym worksheet may be a time-limited activity, and the teens may not be accustomed to thinking positively about themselves, this handout will aid them in using only positive personal attributes.

Once the teens have produced their acronym, they can share it aloud with the group. This is a great opportunity for the teens to see on paper and say aloud positive personal qualities. It is a great way to build their self-esteem!

Positive Personal Attributes

A	Affectionate
	Ambitions
B	Brave
	Bright
C	Calm
	Compassionate
D	Diligent
	Diplomatic
E	Easygoing
	Energetic
F	Faithful
	Friendly
G	Generous
	Gentle
H	Helpful
	Honest
I	Intelligent
	Inventive
J	Joking
	Joyful
K	Kind
	Knowledgeable
L	Loving
	Loyal
M	Magnificent
	Modest
N	Neat
	Nice
O	Optimistic
	Organized
P	Patient
	Polite
Q	Quiet
	Quick-witted
R	Rational
	Reliable
S	Shy
	Sincere
T	Tidy
	Truthful
U	Unassuming
	Understanding
V	Versatile
	Vibrant
W	Warm
	Witty
Y	Yielding
Z	Zany

7(c) Ways to self-soothe

This self-soothe handout coordinates with self-soothe Skill 2 found in Section 3 on distress tolerance skills. The handout provides additional examples for teens to complete their worksheet, using five senses to comfort themselves through stress or pain.

~ *Handout Directions* ~

Give the handout to the teen, along with the "Self-Soothing" worksheet in Section 3 on distress tolerance skills. This handout offers a few ideas for self-soothing with each of the five senses: sight, smell, hear, taste, and touch. The teen can use some of these suggestions to complete their worksheet and for any other ideas unique to them.

Once the teens have completed their worksheets, encourage them to share their lists aloud with one another. Sharing gives the teens a boost of self-esteem, reinforces other teens to work on their DBT skills worksheet, and may offer ideas that the teens had not previously considered.

Self-Soothing List

Ideas for self-soothing from the five senses

SIGHT

- Gaze at nature: flowers, trees, beach, sunrise.
- Look at beautiful pictures online.
- Stargaze at night.
- Watch a burning candle.

SMELL

- Dab on lavender oil.
- Smell the fresh air.
- Make food with soothing smells: coffee, chocolate chip cookies.
- Put on your favorite perfume.

SOUND

- Listen to nature sounds: rain, ocean, waves, birds.
- Sing your favorite song.

TASTE

- Chew fruit-flavored gum or candy.
- Eat your favorite dessert.
- Drink hot tea.

TOUCH

- Take a warm bath or shower.
- Hug your pet or a close friend or family member.
- Wrap up in a soft, fuzzy blanket.
- Get a manicure or pedicure.

7(d) Sleep tight: Suggestions for better sleep

This handout is a list of eight commonly known ways to improve sleep. Teens are notorious for poor sleep habits, going to sleep late, with early awakening for school. These eight ideas suggest how important sleep is for everyone, but especially for those who are emotionally sensitive or who have a mood disorder.

~ *Handout Directions* ~

Provide a handout to the teen alongside your discussion of the emotion regulation skill, PLEASE. This DBT skill is found in Section 4, Skill 6 on emotion regulation: "PLEASE" worksheet. This handout coordinates with the letter "S" in the acronym, PLEASE, and stands for: "Balance Sleep."

Discuss the importance of getting a healthy amount of sleep, and emphasize that the lack of sleep can make teens vulnerable to emotion dysregulation. Ask the teens about their sleep habits and quality of sleep. To further the discussion, ask them, "What suggestions from this list would you be willing to try in order to improve your sleep?"

Sleep Tight

Zzzzzz...

Suggestions for better sleep

1. Stay on a regular sleep schedule—go to sleep and wake up at the same time, daily.
2. Exercise daily—regular exercise helps your body fall asleep at night.
3. Have a comfy bed and pillows.
4. Avoid taking naps—they make it more difficult to fall asleep at bedtime.
5. Avoid alcohol and drugs, including cigarettes.
6. Make sure that your bedroom is comfy—free from outside light or noise.
7. Practice deep breathing at bedtime—regulate your breathing to slow, deep breaths.
8. Avoid caffeine several hours prior to bedtime.

Adapted from Linehan, *DBT Skills Training Manual* (2015b)

7(e) Inspiring statements

The "Inspiring Statements" worksheet is provided to the teens alongside the worksheet, "IMPROVE the Moment," found in Section 3, Skill 4 on distress tolerance. The "Inspiring Statements" worksheet coordinates with the letter "E" from the acronym "IMPROVE," which stands for the word "encouragement."

Encouragement is a strategy for teens to feel inspired during stressful times, replacing negative thoughts and feelings with positive ones. The completed worksheet is an example for the teens. They may use any of the quotes they find helpful in their own worksheet.

The teens will use the blank worksheet to create an individualized page of encouraging quotes, music lyrics, or statements that they find uplifting or supporting to them, so that, in distressing moments, they can go to their completed page and remind themselves of their truths.

Inspiring Statements

You can't calm the storm, so STOP trying.

What you can do is *calm yourself.*

The storm will pass.

~TIMBER HAWKEYE

Stand up for what you believe in, EVEN IF it means standing alone.

You know my name, NOT MY STORY.

Do *small* things with *great love.*

~MOTHER THERESA

The KEY to happiness is letting each situation be what it is instead of what you think it SHOULD be.

~MANDY HALE

Why fit in when you were born to STAND OUT!

~DR. SEUSS

Don't count the days, make the days *count.*

Inspiring Statements

7(f) Reading list

This handout coordinates with Section 3, Skill 3, Wise Mind ACCEPTS. In particular, the reading list is a distracting skill that falls under the letter "A" and stands for "Activities." Activities encourages the teen to fully participate in an activity of their choice which reduces their unhealthy urges or upsetting feelings. This skill is most effective when the teen can be involved in an activity that creates a neutral or opposite feeling to their current negative one.

~ *Worksheet Directions* ~

Provide a worksheet to each teen alongside the handouts and worksheets from the distress tolerance skill, Wise Mind ACCEPTS. Encourage the teens to write a list of the books that they would like to read, which could be a distracting skill when they are experiencing unhealthy urges or any upsetting feelings. Provide time for the teens to share their lists with the group as they may glean ideas from one another's lists.

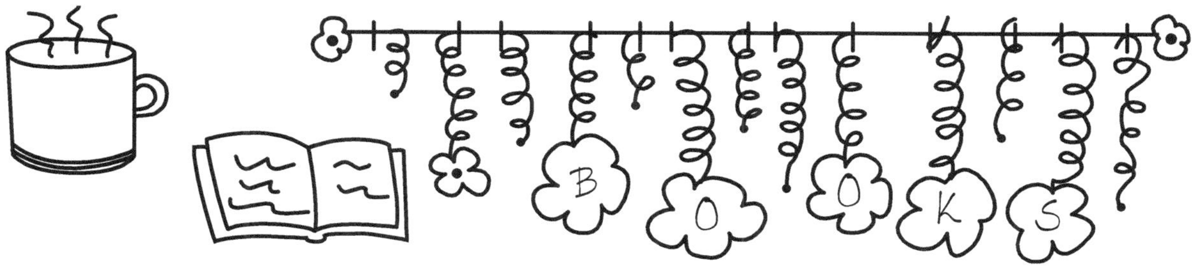

My Reading List:

- Harry Potter—any of them!
- The Clay Lion
- Culloo
- Artemis Fowl

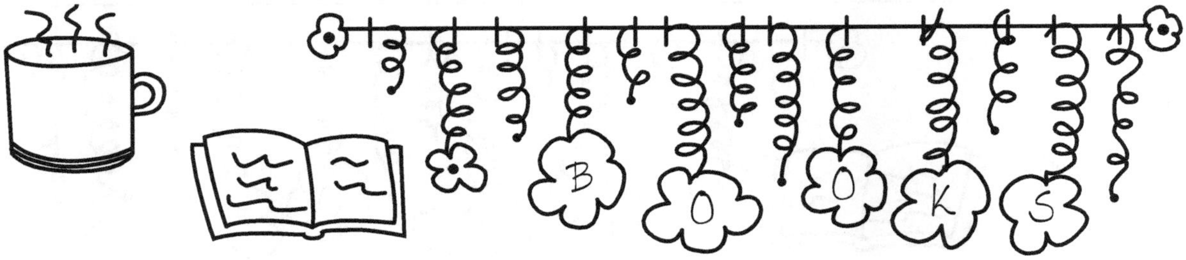

My Reading List:

7(g) Notes

This page provides a space for teens to take notes as you teach them important information about DBT skills and having a life worth living. The notes page encourages teens to take your instruction seriously. It also provides positive peer pressure. Often, when one teen begins to take notes, others tend to follow.

Notes

Section 2

Mindfulness

1. What is Mindfulness (MI)?

Mindfulness is being in the present moment with awareness and acceptance, without judgment of self and others. Linehan (2015b) states that the goals of a mindfulness practice are to: "Reduce suffering and increase happiness, increase control of your mind, and experience reality as it is." Mindfulness is a central concept in DBT and has many benefits, including: being fully present in the moment; becoming less judgmental; increasing self-awareness of thoughts, feelings, behaviors, and body sensations; and maintaining an inner sense of calm. Mindfulness is separated into two parts: WHAT skills and HOW skills.

~ Handout Directions ~

This first mindfulness handout helps the teen to visualize and understand the two parts to mindfulness: WHAT and HOW. This handout further shows the three skills that comprise each of the WHAT and HOW skills.

Mindfulness

mi

WHAT skills

- Observe
- Describe
- Participate

HOW skills

- Non-judgmentally
- One-mindfully
- Effectively

2. WHAT Skills

The WHAT skills, performed one at a time, are the nuts and bolts of what we do in the practice of being mindful. Let's look at the three WHAT skills:

1. *Observe:* Wordless watching with our five senses: see, touch, taste, hear, and smell.
2. *Describe:* Putting words to our observations.
3. *Participate:* The act of being fully engaged in the activity.

~ Worksheet Directions ~

This worksheet has a twofold purpose: to define and explain the WHAT skills to "observe," "describe," and "participate"; and to teach mindfulness through an experiential exercise.

After explaining "observe," "describe," and "participate," do an experiential exercise. For example, let's imagine that you are explaining the WHAT skills with a mindfulness eating exercise. Hand each teen a piece of cinnamon candy or a raisin. Instruct the teens to observe the outside of the candy or raisin with five senses. They can take the candy wrapper off, and again observe with five senses. After eating, they can describe their experience with words. Throughout this exercise, they will remain fully engaged in the activity.

Then, on the worksheet, teens can name the mindfulness activity on the line provided on the right side of the page. In the "Describe with Words" section, they will write what they observed with their senses. In the last section, "Participate," they will rate their level of participation during the activity.

Mindfulness mi

WHAT Skills

1. Observe with five senses, wordless watching. ____________

See   Smell   Taste

Touch   Hear

2. Describe with words...

I see...

I smell...

I taste...

I feel...

I hear...

3. Participate: "I'm gonna give it my all...100%"

Fully throw myself into the experience.
(Rate myself 1–10.) _____

3. HOW Skills

Next are the HOW skills. They are the way in which we practice our WHAT skills. Let's look more closely at the three HOW skills:

1. *One Mindfully:* Being actively attentive to what we are doing in the moment, one thing at a time. The opposite of multitasking.
2. *Non-judgmentally:* Steering our mind away from judgments—good or bad, right or wrong, worthy or unworthy, should or should not. Instead, we want to keep our minds on the facts—who, what, when, where, and how.
3. *Effectively:* Do what works! Acting in an effective manner occurs when a teen does not get caught up in what is fair or unfair, right or wrong, or whether it should or shouldn't be as they are striving to reach a chosen goal.

~ Worksheet Directions ~

This worksheet looks more closely at the HOW skills. Similar to the WHAT worksheet, this worksheet fulfills both technical and experiential explanation and practice. If we continue with the mindful eating exercise, teens can practice being one-mindful, non-judgmental, and effective as they observe, describe, and participate while they eat the candy or raisin.

Mindfulness

mi

HOW Skills

1. Non-judgmentally
   - Just the facts—who, what, where, when, how
   - Don't focus on good/bad, should/shouldn't
2. One-mindfully
   - Do things one at a time
   - No multitasking
   - Focus your mind; practice!
3. Effectively
   - Focus on what works
   - Do what needs to be done to accomplish your goals
   - Let go of revenge
   - Let go of: right/wrong, fair/unfair, should/shouldn't

Adapted from Linehan, *DBT Skills Training Manual* (2015b)

4. Mindfulness Activities

In a mindfulness practice, the teen is in the present moment with awareness and acceptance without judgment of self and others. Because mindfulness is a practice, it is helpful for the teen to have a list of mindfulness activities to practice on a daily basis. Your teen can use the following handouts. Remind the teens that regular practice of mindfulness helps them to be successful as they use it in upsetting situations.

~ *Handout Directions* ~

The first handout teaches mindful breathing. Starfish breathing is adapted from the "Five-Finger Meditation" in *Planting Seeds: Practicing Mindfulness with Children* (2011) by Thich Nhat Hanh and the Plum Village Community with permission of Parallax Press, Berkeley, California (www.parallax.org).

Describe starfish breathing in the following way: Make a starfish with one outstretched hand; spread your fingers out wide. Use your pointer finger to trace along the outline of each finger starting at the base of the thumb. Bring awareness to your breathing and breathe in, move the pointer finger up the finger, and then exhale as you move the finger down the other side. Keep tracing each finger, and following with your breath, until ending at the base of the pinkie finger.

Mindfulness Activity

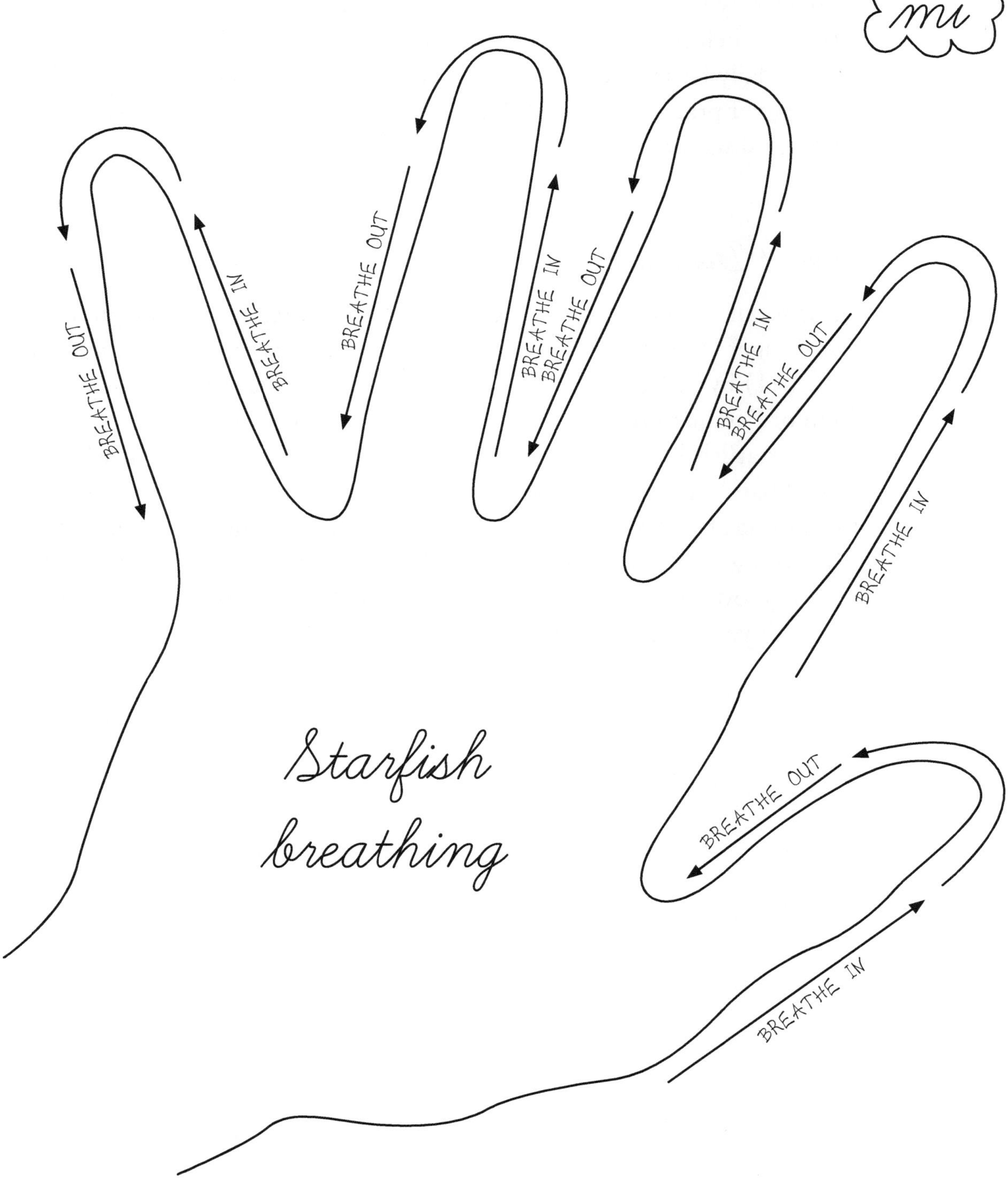

Adapted from the "Five Finger Meditation" in *Planting Seeds: Practicing Mindfulness with Children* (2011) by Thich Nhat Hanh and the Plum Village Community with permission of Parallax Press, Berkeley, CA (www.parallax.org)

~ Handout Directions ~

The next mindful breathing exercise is called "Square Breathing." This exercise can be done in several ways:

1. Follow the directions on the worksheet.
2. Locate any four-sided object: box, frame, piece of paper, or window. Instruct the teen to start with their gaze or pointer finger on the top-left corner of the square object and inhale; move the finger to the top-right corner.

   Pause and move the gaze or finger to the bottom-right corner.

   Exhale and move the gaze or finger to the left-bottom corner.

   Pause again and lift the gaze or finger to the top-left corner.

   Instruct the teen to repeat the instructions four times.
3. Another way to do this activity is to count the corners of the square, or to say (or think) calming words. Follow the instructions above, and count or add words as you progress from one corner to another.

   For example, begin your gaze or finger on the top-left corner of the square, inhale and say, "One" or "Peace."

   Pause, move your gaze or finger to the bottom-right corner and say, "Two" or "Joy." Exhale and bring the gaze or finger to the left-bottom corner and say, "Three" or "Trust."

   Pause again and move the gaze or finger to the top-left corner and say, "Four" or "Hope."

   Repeat the instructions four times.

Mindfulness Activity

Follow the SQUARE to calm

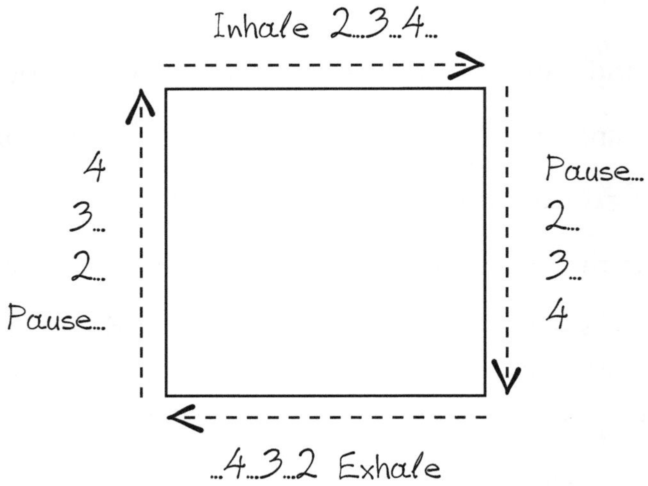

S·q·u·a·r·e breathing

1. Inhale through your nose to the count of 4.
2. Pause to the count of 4.
3. Exhale through your mouth to the count of 4.
4. Pause to the count of 4.
5. Repeat 4 times.

This exercise can be done with any 4-sided object!

~ Handout Directions ~

This handout is a list of ten mindfulness activities for teens to practice. They can add mindfulness activities to this list as they learn new ones, or they can add them to a blank "Notes" page found in Section 1, Skill 7(g).

Ten Ways to P·r·a·c·t·i·c·e Mindfulness

mi

1. Write calligraphy.
2. The telephone game.
3. Hold a feather. Mindfully describe with five senses.
4. Eat a raisin, chocolate, or mint. Mindfully describe with five senses.
5. Listen to a meditation bell—notice when the sound ends.
6. List all the songs, food, countries, etc. that begin with the letter ____.
7. Listen to a favorite song. Name emotions that arise.
8. List movies that are ____ (drama, comedy, suspense) genre.
9. Walk and measure your footsteps. Align your breathing to your steps, making them short and slow.
10. Listen to all the sounds around you. Describe what you heard.

Adapted from Linehan, *DBT Skills Training Manual* (2015b)

5. Grounding Techniques

The next two worksheets are grounding techniques. Grounding techniques use the five senses to focus attention on the here and now.

~ *Worksheet Directions* ~

On the next two worksheets, follow the written directions to practice grounding. Grounding techniques work best in a challenging moment when teens have been practicing them on a routine basis.

mi

Grounding with Five Senses

1. Sit comfortably.

2. Observe your breathing and its pattern: inhale, exhale, and pause.

3. Observe your five senses and be in the present moment:

   - What are five things you see?

   - What are four things you can feel with touch?

   - What are three things you hear?

   - What are two things you smell?

   - What is one thing you taste?

Adapted from Linehan, *DBT Skills Training Manual* (2015b)

mi

Five Senses 5

1. Sit comfortably.

2. Observe your breathing and its pattern: inhale, exhale, and pause.

3. Observe your five senses and be in the present moment. Give a moment to each.

- HEAR—What are the sounds around you or internally, like your breathing?
- SMELL—What are the smells in the moment?
- SEE—Pay attention closely. What do you see around you?
- TASTE—Notice any tastes in your mouth.
- TOUCH—Pay attention to any sensation coming into contact with your skin.

Adapted from Linehan, *DBT Skills Training Manual* (2015b)

6. Coloring Sheets

Teens can practice mindfulness through doodling or coloring. The following two worksheets are coloring pages that I created and have used many times in my teen DBT groups. Teen boys and girls love coloring pages, and it is by far one of their favorite ways to practice mindfulness.

~ *Worksheet Directions* ~

Provide each teen with a coloring sheet. Make sure to have crayons, markers, or colored pencils available to them. Instruct the teens to use their HOW and WHAT skills while they color. Following their period of mindfulness, encourage the teens to describe what they observed.

7. Three States of Mind

In DBT, there are three states of mind: "emotion mind," "reasonable mind," and "wise mind." We strive to spend most of our time in "wise mind," where we are in balance between "emotion mind" and "reasonable mind." The following are further explanations of the three states of mind:

> Emotion mind is thought of as being "hot." In emotion mind, the teen's emotions are in control, and they are not using rational thought to stay in balance. When a teen is in an "extreme" state of emotion mind, they tend to be emotionally reactive. Professions which rely on emotion may include an artist or a writer.
>
> Reasonable mind is "cool," and logic leads behavior. When a person is stuck in "extreme" reasonable mind, they may have difficulty engaging their emotions and become detached or uncaring. Individuals whose strengths lie in reasoning may have occupations in the sciences or mathematics.
>
> In wise mind, people are in balance with their thoughts and emotions. In wise mind, people are in touch with their intuition, and can reflect on their experience and common sense. Those who have the occupation of physician or therapist are in wise mind as they work.

~ *Worksheet Directions* ~

Provide a worksheet to each teen. Use the worksheet to describe the three states of mind. Point out the three images to further illustrate them. Reasonable mind is pictured by a thinking bubble; emotion mind is depicted by a heart; and wise mind is illustrated by a wise owl. The table at the bottom of the worksheet expresses possible occupations and extremes of each mind.

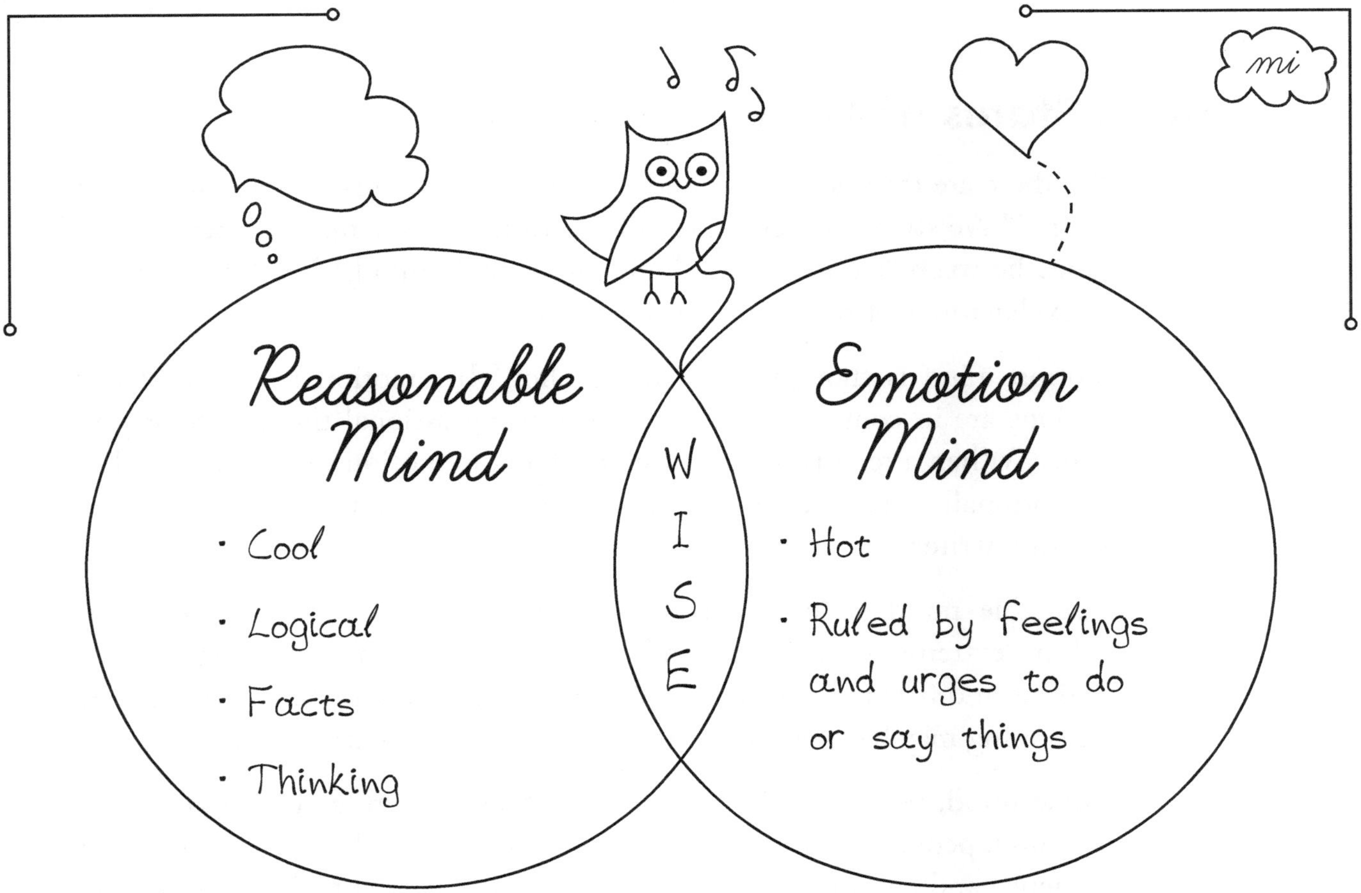

WISE MIND: Balance between emotion and reasonable minds. Recognize and respect your feelings and respond in a calm way.

	Reasonable	Wise	Emotion
JOBS:	Attorney	Teacher	Artist
	Computer programmer	Doctor	Writer
EXTREME:	Uncaring	Intuitive	Out of control emotion and/ or behavior
	Detached	Wisdom	

Adapted from Linehan, *DBT Skills Training Manual* (2015b)

Section 3

Distress Tolerance

1. What is Distress Tolerance (DT)?

Distress tolerance (DT) is the second module or group of skills to teach to the teens. Teens use distress tolerance skills when it is difficult or nearly impossible to change a situation or their emotions, and to tolerate emotional or physical pain.

There are two primary skill sets within distress tolerance:

> *Crisis survival* skills help teens to tolerate stress and life's frustrations, and then to actively problem-solve through the moment without making the situation worse. This set of skills helps the teen to avoid impulsive behaviors that may result in additional or exacerbated problems.
>
> *Reality acceptance* skills teach teens to identify when things are out of their control, and when they are unable to find an immediate solution to their problem. These skills focus on teens accepting themselves, the fact, feeling, or situation as it is without trying to change it or avoid it. Reality acceptance skills offer a temporary remedy from emotions, situations, or facts that cannot be changed in the near future, if at all.

These skills are extremely important for teens as life often gives us unavoidable and difficult situations and emotions, and they have to learn to deal with them. Attempting to avoid situations causes the situation or feelings to worsen over time.

As a visual cue, each handout or worksheet will have a "dt" symbol on the page, typically in the top-right corner, to remind the teens that the skill comes from the distress tolerance module.

~ Handout Directions ~

This handout is an introduction to distress tolerance skills. Again, the handout is utilizing visual cues in order to enhance further learning of the concepts. The handout guides the skills trainer in defining distress tolerance, and its two sets of skills: crisis survival and radical acceptance. Each skill is visually separated and defined on the page.

In addition, the handout also provides an introductory list of distress tolerance skills that we will be learning and practicing in the activity manual. There is room at the bottom of the page to add any additional distress tolerance skills for your teen.

What is Distress Tolerance?

dt

Crisis survival & **Reality acceptance**

- Self-soothing
- Wise Mind ACCEPTS
- IMPROVE the moment
- The STOP skill
- TIP skills
- Pros and cons

- Willingness vs. willfulness
- Turning the mind
- Radical acceptance
- Half-smiling

2. Crisis Survival Skills: Self-Soothing

In self-soothing, teens engage in activities that will bring comfort, gentleness, and nurturance into their life during a difficult experience or feeling. In general, self-soothing helps the teen to manage through their pain while avoiding an impulsive action that may make the situation worse.

~ *Worksheet Directions* ~

Provide the worksheet to the teen along with the coordinating handout "Self-Soothing List" which is found in Section 1, Skill 7(c). The handout provides examples of self-soothing for teens to complete their worksheet.

Describe the self-soothing skill; provide examples of comforting and nurturing activities or objects in each category of the five senses.

Encourage the teen to be creative and ponder on what is uniquely comforting and gentle to them. Remind them that their completed list of self-soothing strategies is for them to use and no one else!

In a group setting, ask the teens to share their individual lists as they may name strategies that will benefit another group member. Positively reinforce each member's sharing.

Self-Soothing

dt

Self-soothe with five senses when you're dealing with a lot of stress. It helps you stay in the moment, and feel comforted.

SIGHT

- Pictures of my friends
- Pictures of sunset or watching it
- Roses

SMELL

- Warm vanilla sugar lotion
- Fruity gum
- Smell of chocolate chip cookies

SOUND

- Birds singing
- White noise—fan!
- Ocean waves

TASTE

- Cinnamon
- Cake—any flavor
- Hot chocolate

TOUCH

- Fluffy blankets
- Soft flannel
- Hug my puppy

Self-Soothing

dt

Self-soothe with five senses when you're dealing with a lot of stress. It helps you stay in the moment, and feel comforted.

SIGHT

SOUND

SMELL

TASTE

TOUCH

3. Crisis Survival Skills: Wise Mind ACCEPTS

ACCEPTS is a DBT distress tolerance skill. The acronym, "ACCEPTS," stands for seven distracting skills. Teens use ACCEPTS skills in a crisis situation (conflict with a teacher or parent, break-up with a boyfriend or girlfriend), and guides them in using healthy distractions. These skills help teens to avoid damaging coping skills, such as: alcohol, drugs, or cigarettes; self-cutting or skin-picking; isolation; oversleeping; excessive use of technology (computer, phone, video games); overeating; and suicidal thinking.

The seven sets of distracting skills include: Activities, Contributing, Comparisons, Emotions, Pushing Away, Thoughts, and Sensations. When teens mindfully practice these seven skills, it gives them a short break from the situation to calm, and then later return, to solve the problem. Let's look further at each of the seven distracting skills:

1. **A**ctivities: When teens fully participate in an activity, it reduces their unhealthy urges and upsetting feelings. This skill is most effective when the teen can be involved in an activity that creates a neutral or opposite feeling to their current negative one. Some examples of activities to engage in include: hobbies (garden, collect baseball cards, knit, crochet, scrapbook, pokemon cards, or dog-training); sports (tennis, gymnastics, basketball, baseball, soccer, swimming, dance, lacrosse, bowling, biking, track or cross-country running); movies (comedy, drama, mystery, horror, or another genre); books or magazines (non-fiction or fiction); and crossword or sudoku puzzles.

2. **C**ontributing: Doing something thoughtful or helpful for themselves or others. When teens focus their thoughts on serving others or doing something helpful for themselves, it distracts them from their own emotional pain. Some ideas include: volunteer work at a local organization (humane society, meals for elderly, boys and girls clubs); help a neighbor (mow their grass or clear the snow off their driveway); babysit for a family friend; or volunteer to help at a church or religious organization.

3. **C**omparisons: Teens compare their situation to others who are coping in the same way or not as well as themselves. Also, teens can compare to times in the past, knowing that their current coping and situation are in a better place. Another strategy is to compare themselves to those who are generally less fortunate. Although this skill can be helpful, it is not satisfying for

everyone. Teens may note others who have less family support or who have more severe emotional or physical health problems.

4. **E**motions: Teens can participate in an activity that brings up opposite emotions to their current negative one. For example, watch a funny or suspenseful movie when feeling sad, or listen to upbeat music or watch a silly TV show when feeling angry.

5. **P**ushing Away: In a crisis, teens can temporarily repress their feelings of the situation. As an example, instruct the teen to imagine a solid, shatterproof glass between themselves and the situation; or imagine shrinking the situation and putting it into a locked box on a shelf.

6. **T**houghts: Teens can distract themselves with busy thoughts to keep their pain at bay. Some suggestions are: count by 3s or 5s, say the ABCs backward, do a crossword puzzle or a seek-n-find, walk and count steps or cracks in the sidewalk, and name the make of cars or states of license plates on the road.

7. **S**ensations: Teens can distract by changing their focus from their upset to physical sensations in their body. Some ideas include: hold an ice pack or a cold washcloth to their neck, forehead, or chest; take a hot or cold shower; eat a popsicle, drink a cold or hot beverage; listen to loud music; sit in a hot tub.

~ Handout Directions ~

Provide a handout to each of the teens. Use the above information as well as other sources to explain the distress tolerance skill, "Wise Mind ACCEPTS." Remind the teens that the "dt" icon in the upper-right corner signifies that ACCEPTS belongs in the "distress tolerance" category of skills.

Wise Mind ACCEPTS

dt

Activities: fully participate in an activity that creates a neutral/opposite feeling (gardening, watch a movie).

Contributing: do something thoughtful or helpful for yourself or others (volunteer, mow my neighbor's grass).

Comparisons: compare my situation to others, or to my coping in the past.

Emotions: engaging in an activity that brings up emotions that are opposite to current ones (watch a funny video when I'm sad).

Pushing away: physically or emotionally block painful situations or emotions (imagine putting my pain in a box).

Thoughts: distract yourself with other, busy thoughts (count by 3s, say ABCs backwards).

Sensations: change focus from feeling upset with physical sensations (hold ice, sit in a hot tub).

Adapted from Linehan, *DBT Skills Training Manual* (2015b)

~ Worksheet Directions ~

Once you have reviewed the ACCEPTS skill, provide each teen with a blank and completed worksheet. In addition, provide the handout from Section 1, Skill 7(f), "Reading List," to coordinate with the letter "A" in "Activities." For those who enjoy reading, it is a great way to distract from painful feelings.

Instruct the teens to identify an example or two (or more) of each of the seven distraction skills. Once the teens have completed their worksheet, encourage them to share their ideas with one another. This promotes further learning and brainstorming successful ways to use the ACCEPTS skill.

Wise Mind ACCEPTS

A **Activities:** working out with weights and the treadmill, read *Harry Potter* series.

C **Contributing:** volunteer to tutor at school, say "Hi" to kids sitting alone at lunch or invite them to sit with me.

C **Comparing:** compare my feelings now to last year when I was depressed.

E **Emotions:** watch funny YouTube videos, listen to praise music.

P **Pushing away:** put my hurtful memories into an imaginary box...for a while.

T **Thoughts:** do a crossword puzzle, count by 3s.

S **Sensations:** hold ice in my mouth, squeeze a ball really hard.

dt

Wise Mind ACCEPTS

A Activities:

C Contributing:

C Comparing:

E Emotions:

P Pushing away:

T Thoughts:

S Sensations:

dt

4. Crisis Survival Skills: IMPROVE the Moment

IMPROVE the moment, a distress tolerance skill, is used when teens feel overwhelmed in a crisis. In the moment, they are replacing negative feelings and situations with positive ones. The acronym stands for:

1. **I**magery: Use imagery to distract, soothe, or cope with an upsetting feeling or situation. The teens can imagine an upsetting situation concluding with a positive ending, or they can imagine handling a stressful situation well.
2. **M**eaning: Find or create purpose, meaning, or value in a painful situation. Encourage teens to consider, "What can I learn from this situation?" and "Can I grow from this experience in any way?" Meaning helps teens to find the blessing as they endure difficult times.
3. **P**rayer: Teens can ask for strength and wisdom to get through tough situations or feelings. This is a skill to tolerate the moment rather than asking, "Why me?" or asking for the pain to go away.
4. **R**elaxation: Teens can relax their body during times of stress. Calming the body provides the teen with a moment of space to use other DBT skills.
5. **O**ne Thing at a Time: Teens previously learned this skill in mindfulness. In "one thing at a time," teens focus on getting through this one crisis or one moment, rather than dwelling on past events or future worries.

   In addition, this skill reminds teens to break overwhelming tasks into smaller, manageable portions. Doing one thing at a time makes it easier to tolerate situations and to arrive at a successful outcome.
6. **V**acation: Teens learn to take short breaks as they deal with stress or crises. Vacations typically last from 10 minutes to 2 hours.
7. **E**ncouragement: In encouragement, teens say helpful, uplifting comments, quotes, or music lyrics to themselves.

~ Handout Directions ~

Provide a handout to each teen. Use the above information to explain the distress tolerance skill, IMPROVE the moment. Discuss each letter, what it stands for, and its meaning. As you review each letter, brainstorm with the teens and compile a list of possible examples corresponding to each letter to be used in the following worksheets.

Improve... the Moment

dt

Imagery: use imagery to cope with an upsetting feeling or situation; imagine a positive outcome (imagine being at the beach, imagine handling frustration well).

Meaning: find meaning in a painful situation; consider, "What can I learn from this situation?"

Prayer: ask for strength or wisdom to get through a tough situation.

Relaxation: calm your body during stressful times (listen to a guided meditation, practice square breathing).

One thing in the moment: focus your mind on getting through just this one moment or crisis.

Vacation: take short breaks as you deal with stress—from 10 minutes to 2 hours (take a short nap, drink a latte).

Encouragement: say uplifting things to yourself ("I've got this!" or "I did a great job!").

Adapted from Linehan, *DBT Skills Training Manual* (2015b)

~ Worksheet Directions ~

Hand a worksheet to each teen. Provide a blank sheet and a completed one. In addition, provide the coordinating worksheet, "Inspiring Statements," found in Section 1, Skill 7(e), to each teen. The inspiring statements worksheet coordinates to the letter "E"—which stands for encouragement, from the acronym, "IMPROVE."

Review the IMPROVE skill. Remind the teens of the skill and the list that they previously created.

Instruct the teens to continue making their own list of strategies that coordinates with the eight skills within IMPROVE.

Once the teens have completed their worksheet, encourage them to share ideas with one another. As the teens share, validate their lists and efforts to successfully use the skill. The following vignette is reflected in the completed worksheet.

Vignette

18-year-old Dylan just left home to begin his first semester of college. He is excited to be away at college and he's also feeling overwhelmed and lonely.

IMPROVE

…the Moment

Imagery: Imagine doing well in classes and meeting new friends. Imagine my favorite spot at the cove.

Meaning: Reflect on how much I'll learn in classes, and grow into an independent person.

Prayer: Ask for strength to bear the pain; turn things over to God or another higher power.

Relaxation: Listen to relaxing music, take a hot bath, and practice deep breathing.

One thing in the moment: Pay attention to the moment while in classes or with friends, and stay focused on my school work.

Vacation: Take short naps, take coffee breaks, have short conversations with my friends back home.

Encouragement: Repeat, "I'll be OK." Or, "I can do it!"

IMPROVE

…the Moment

Imagery:

Meaning:

Prayer:

Relaxation:

One thing in the moment:

Vacation:

Encouragement:

5. Crisis Survival Skills: The STOP Skill

STOP, a distress tolerance skill, is an acronym and stands for:

S = stop, T = take a step back, O = observe, and P = proceed mindfully.

STOP helps teens to stop and think before impulsively saying or doing something that they will later regret.

Let's look more closely at each letter:

1. **S**top: Teens need to stop completely when they notice a strong emotion and where there is a chance that they may react impulsively. This eliminates the urge to react in ways that could result in harmful (to themselves or others) behavior or comments.
2. **T**ake a step back: This pause gives the teen a moment to step back (figuratively or literally), and think through ways to solve the situation.
3. **O**bserve: Next, the teen mindfully observes themselves, others, and their environment. They can ask, "What am I (or another) doing or saying?" It is also a time to gather facts and information.
4. **P**roceed Mindfully: Now, the teen can begin to move forward, in a mindful way, to solve the situation. They can ask, "How can I be effective and make the situation better?"

~ Handout Directions ~

Provide a handout to each teen. Use the handout, the above information as well as other sources to explain the STOP skill. Use the acronym to discuss each letter and explain its meaning. Point out the visual cues on the pages so as to enhance their memory of each step in the skill.

STOP!

______ Skill

Stop

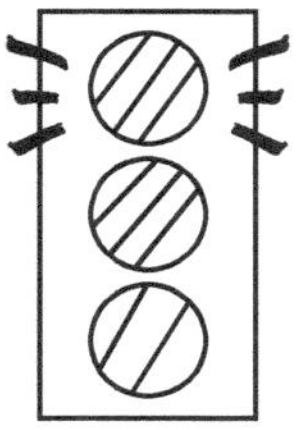

Freeze!
Don't act on my feelings or urges.

Take a step back

literally or figuratively.
Don't let my feelings take over.

Observe

within and around me.
Gather facts and information.

Proceed

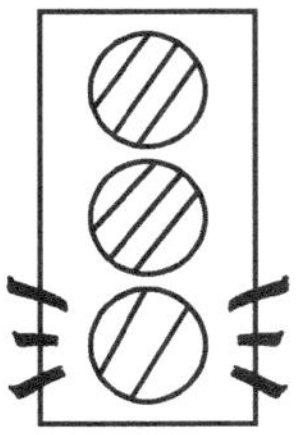

"go"
Mindfully move forward to solve the problem.

Adapted from Linehan, *DBT Skills Training Manual* (2015b)

~ Worksheet Directions ~

Hand out a worksheet to each teen. Review the STOP skill, or engage the teens to recall each letter of the skill and its meaning.

In this worksheet, use a combination of discussion and role plays. The teens will use role plays to practice the STOP skill as the most effective way to build a new habit is to repeatedly perform the behavior. The teens can offer situations to role-play, or you can use the following ideas:

> You're walking down the hallway at school, and a peer calls you an unkind name.
>
> You're at a football game. One of your close friends is in an argument with her boyfriend. He accuses her of cheating and cusses at her.
>
> You're at home relaxing and watching a movie in the family room. Your younger sibling comes into the room, playing a loud video game, refusing to turn it down.
>
> Your teacher gave you a zero on a homework paper. You know you turned in the homework. You talk to her, and she insists that she never received it.
>
> At school, you make plans with some friends for the weekend. That evening, your parents inform you that your cousins are coming into town for the weekend. They demand that you cancel your plans in order that you attend a family function.

Stop STOP Skill

Stop

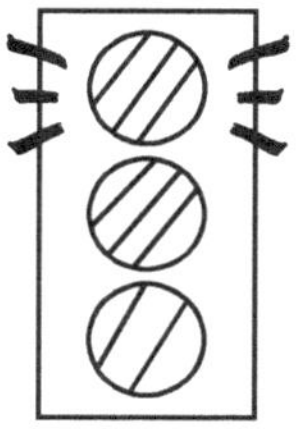

Name a situation that may cause you to react impulsively, making the situation worse.

- Role-play; practice freezing.

Take a step back

- Role-play physically taking a step back and a deep breath to calm down.

Observe

Ask myself:

- What are my thoughts and feelings?
- What is the situation?
- What are others saying and doing?

Proceed

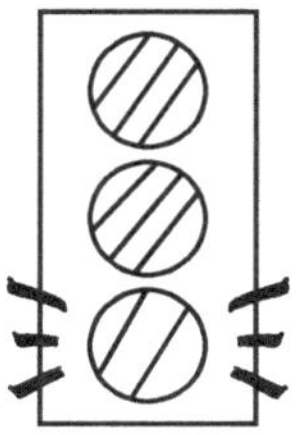

Ask myself:

- What do I want from this situation?
- What are my goals in this situation?
- What choices might make this situation better or worse?

Adapted from Linehan, *DBT Skills Training Manual* (2015b)

6. Crisis Survival Skills: TIP Skills

TIP is a distress tolerance, crisis survival skill by Linehan (2015b). TIP is an acronym and stands for:

T = tip the body temperature, I = intense exercise, and P = paced breathing.

When teens use TIP skills, it quickly regulates their body, which, in turn leads to a faster regulation of their emotions. TIP skills are easy to do, and do not require a lot of thinking. At the same time, they are an effective tool for teens. Let's look more closely at each of them:

1. Tip the body **T**emperature: Tip the body temperature by holding ice, ice packs, or bags of frozen vegetables on the eyes, face, neck, or chest.
2. **I**ntense Exercise: Do intense aerobic exercise for 20 minutes. Exercise is well known to have a positive effect on mood and self-esteem. Intense exercise causes deep breathing, and helps teens to further regulate their emotions.
3. **P**aced breathing: Paced breathing helps to slow down breathing which regulates the teen's emotions. Two ways to practice paced breathing are starfish and square breathing found in Section 2, Skill 4, of mindfulness activities.

~ *Worksheet Directions* ~

Provide a worksheet for each teen. Explain TIP skills using the above information and other sources. Instruct teens to write strategies on the worksheet that they are willing to practice and use when they feel intense emotions.

As a group, discuss strategies within each letter or skill. As a group, practice different strategies: holding ice to the face, neck, eyes; and paced breathing.

Change Your Body Chemistry

TIP (← skills)

T TIP THE TEMPERATURE OF YOUR BODY

- Hold an ice pack on your face.
- Take a cold bath or shower.

I INTENSE EXERCISE

20 minutes of: burpees, jumping jacks, jogging, lifting weights, or fast walking.

P PACED BREATHING

Practice deep breathing: starfish and square breathing.

dt

Adapted from Linehan, *DBT Skills Training Manual* (2015b)

Change Your Body Chemistry

(← skills)

T TIP THE TEMPERATURE OF YOUR BODY

I INTENSE EXERCISE

P PACED BREATHING

dt

Adapted from Linehan, *DBT Skills Training Manual* (2015b)

7. Crisis Survival Skills: Pros and Cons

"Pros and Cons" is a distress tolerance skill for teens to use as they make decisions. The grid looks at both the advantages and disadvantages of options and tolerating pain; avoiding harmful behavior; and acting impulsively.

In Pros and Cons, teens think through the negative and positive outcomes (both long term and short term), while giving them a moment to avoid acting on impulsive urges. Teens can also use the grid to think ahead before an urge hits, and write out the pros and cons of the situation. Afterward, they can carry the list with them as a reminder of the outcome, and the decision they chose from using the skill.

~ *Worksheet Directions* ~

Provide a worksheet for each teen and explain the Pros and Cons skill. Instruct the teens to write a list of problems or emotionally upsetting situations. Ask the teens to choose situations in which they would find it challenging to tolerate pain, avoid harmful behavior, or not act impulsively on an urge.

From the list of problems, instruct the teens to choose one item to practice using pros and cons. First, teens will list pros and cons for acting on the problem behavior or urge. Next, they will list pros and cons of resisting the problem behavior or crisis urge. The teens can consider short-term and long-term outcomes.

In a group setting, teens can share their "Pros and Cons" worksheets. This is an opportunity for teens to share problem-solving solutions with one another.

The following vignette is used to illustrate the Pros and Cons skill in the completed worksheet.

Vignette

Meredith is a 14-year-old 9th grader. She is invited to a party in the neighborhood by Samantha. They've been friends since the age of five. Most of Meredith's friends are going to the party, but she's heard that there will be a lot of older kids there, too.

Meredith thinks that the party will be fun, but she's worried about drinking and drug use. She and her parents are completely opposed to it. If she goes to the party, she will have to sneak out of her house and break family rules.

Several of Meredith's friends are encouraging her to go. One of her close friends, AJ, isn't going, and he's invited her to go to the movies instead.

Meredith decides to fill out a Pros and Cons sheet to consider all of her options and make the wisest choice for herself.

Pros and Cons

dt

	Pros	Cons
ACTING ON THE URGE—GO TO THE PARTY	(pros of acting on urges, giving up, or avoiding what needs to be done) · My friends will be there. · I'll meet new people. · It should be fun!	(cons of acting on urges, giving in, giving up, or avoiding what needs to be done) · My parents will probably find out. · I'll get grounded. · I'll lose my parents' trust. · I'll let AJ down.
RESISTING THE URGE—DON'T GO TO THE PARTY	(pros of resisting urges, doing what needs to be done, and not giving up) · I won't have to worry about how to say "no" to drinking/doing drugs. · I can go to the movies with AJ. · I'll be building trust with my parents.	(cons of resisting urges, doing what needs to be done, and not giving up) · I'll miss out on fun. · I won't meet people who are going. · I'll miss being with my friends.

Write out your pros and cons, and carry them with you.

Adapted from Linehan, *DBT Skills Training Manual* (2015b)

Pros and Cons

dt

	Pros	Cons
ACTING ON THE URGE	(pros of acting on urges, giving up, or avoiding what needs to be done)	(cons of acting on urges, giving in, giving up, or avoiding what needs to be done)
RESISTING THE URGE	(pros of resisting urges, doing what needs to be done, and not giving up)	(cons of resisting urges, doing what needs to be done, and not giving up)

Write out your pros and cons, and carry them with you.

Adapted from Linehan, *DBT Skills Training Manual* (2015b)

8. Reality Acceptance Skills: Willingness vs. Willfulness

"Willingness vs. Willfulness" is a distress tolerance, reality acceptance skill. In life, some situations, facts, and feelings are distasteful, and we have to learn to accept them anyway. Acceptance does not mean that we like it, it just means that we accept it. Teens must learn to notice when they are being willing or willful, and replace willful with willing responses.

- Willfulness is:
  - » Fighting against yourself, others, or the world.
  - » Trying to change a situation that cannot be changed, or refusing to make changes that are needed.
  - » Insisting on being in control; wanting things to "go my way."
  - » Saying, "No" or "Yes, but…"
- Willingness is:
  - » Being open to doing what needs to be done.
  - » Acknowledging the reality of the situation.
  - » Doing what needs to be done with an accepting heart and attitude.
  - » Being flexible and not fighting against reality.

~ *Handout Directions* ~

Give a handout to each teen. Use the top portion of the handout (as well as the above explanation and other sources) to explain the DBT distress tolerance, reality acceptance skill of Willingness vs. Willfulness.

Next, use the bottom half of the handout to guide the teens in being mindful, and noticing willingness and willfulness in themselves.

First, instruct the teens to imagine a time when they experienced *willfulness*: refusing to follow a rule at home or school, refusing to do homework, or arguing with someone; and *willingness*: saying "Okay" when a parent says "No," offering to do an unpleasant chore, and getting homework done and turned in on time.

Then, ask the teens to describe their thoughts, feelings, body posture, words, and tone of voice that correspond to their experience of willingness and willfulness.

Encourage the teens to share their examples of willfulness and willingness. Allow the teens time to share examples of their thoughts, feelings, body posture, words, and tone of voice. As the teens share together, they may identify with another's example of their personal experience of willingness and willfulness.

Willingness vs. Willfulness

dt

- Being open to doing what needs to be done.
- Doing it with an accepting heart and attitude.
- Being flexible not fighting against reality.

- Fighting against myself, others, or the world.
- Trying to stay in control.
- Wanting things to "go my way."
- Saying, "No" or "Yes, but..."

Notice and describe examples of each: describe my thoughts, feelings, body posture, words, and tone of voice:

Willingness

- Open hands
- Palms up
- Calm and open
- Say, "Okay"

Willfulness

- Closed hand, fist
- Crossed arms
- Angry
- Say, "No!"

Adapted from Linehan, *DBT Skills Training Manual* (2015b)

Willingness vs. Willfulness

dt

- Being open to doing what needs to be done.
- Doing it with an accepting heart and attitude.
- Being flexible not fighting against reality.

- Fighting against myself, others, or the world.
- Trying to stay in control.
- Wanting things to "go my way."
- Saying, "No" or "Yes, but..."

Notice and describe examples of each: describe my thoughts, feelings, body posture, words, and tone of voice:

Willingness	Willfulness
•	•
•	•
•	•
•	•

Adapted from Linehan, *DBT Skills Training Manual* (2015b)

~ Worksheet Directions ~

Review the concepts of willingness vs. willfulness or, alternatively, encourage a teen to review the concepts with the group.

Provide a worksheet for each teen. This worksheet outlines the steps to replace willfulness with willingness.

First, discuss each step to replace willfulness with willingness. Use the vignette provided below, another example, or one previously discussed to practice steps 1–4 together. Another optional exercise is to role-play the example.

Note: Step 4 on the worksheet describes the skill, Willing Hands, which reflects the body's acceptance of reality. This skill is often taught and practiced alongside the skill, Half-Smiling, which is found in Section 3 here, Skill 11.

Vignette

John is a 13-year-old boy. He lives with his mom, dad, and older sister, Penny. Typically, John gets stuck in willfulness when his parents ask him to help with chores around the house. Often, John doesn't want to stop playing to do chores, and he gets angry when his parents demand it.

On the completed worksheet, teens can see answers to, "How would John observe and describe his willfulness?"

Replace Willfulness with... Willingness → Step by Step

dt

1. Notice willfulness, describe it:

   My thoughts: "Why do I have to do it?"

   My feelings: angry, irritated

   My body: fists, loud walking

   My words or tone of voice: loud voice—almost yelling, mean and hurtful words

2. Radically and non-judgmentally accept my willfulness. I notice I'm fighting against doing chores.

3. Turn my mind to willingness, over and over. Say to myself: "I'm accepting this situation as it is."

4. Practice a willing, open posture.

   - Uncross my arms, drop them to my sides and open my hands, palms up.

Adapted from Linehan, *DBT Skills Training Manual* (2015b)

dt

Replace Willfulness with... Willingness → Step by Step

1. Notice willfulness, describe it:

   My thoughts:

   My feelings:

   My body:

   My words or tone of voice:

2. Radically and non-judgmentally accept my willfulness. I notice:

3. Turn my mind to willingness, over and over. Say to myself:

4. Describe a willing, open posture.

   .

Adapted from Linehan, *DBT Skills Training Manual* (2015b)

9. Reality Acceptance Skills: Turning the Mind

Turning the mind is a distress tolerance skill. The concept is easy, and the practice is hard! In the skill, teens practice accepting a reality that feels unacceptable.

Accepting an unacceptable reality takes effort and choice. The more painful the situation, the more the teen will need to repeatedly turn their mind...many times a day, hour, or even minute.

Turning the mind incorporates four steps:

1. *Observe that you are no longer accepting*: Teens notice when they are not accepting something. Encourage teens to check inside for their individual cues of not accepting: noticing thoughts, feelings, body sensations, facial expressions, and tone of voice.

2. *Make an inner commitment to accept reality as it is*: Teens go inside, make a choice to accept reality, and turn their mind to accepting. They can imagine physically turning to acceptance.

3. *Do it again, over and over*: Steps 1 and 2 often need repeating. It's okay! The more painful the situation, the more it will need to be repeated.

4. *Develop a plan for catching yourself out of acceptance*: Teens can think ahead and plan for the future times when they are not accepting. Questions to consider: How can they learn from past times to prepare better for the future? Is there a situation they find challenging? If so, teens can plan ahead, catch themselves out of acceptance, and be ready!

~ Handout Directions ~

Provide a handout for each teen. Teach turning the mind DBT skill using the above information and other sources.

As you review the steps, point out the visual cues on the page:

> Turning the mind starts at a fork in the road, with a choice between accepting and rejecting reality. The fork in the road, drawn on the page, illustrates the two choices.
>
> Choosing the acceptance road has a positive outcome in life. Thus, the end of the acceptance road shows a doodle of a relaxing day of sunshine and birds.

Choosing the rejection road ends poorly in life, as depicted by the image of a broken heart.

In step 2, the teens make an inner commitment to turn to acceptance. On the handout, there is a rock pathway leading from the rejection road to the acceptance road. Teens can use this picture to imagine choosing this path at any point…they have a choice to leave the rejection road and move themselves over to the acceptance road.

Turning the Mind

dt

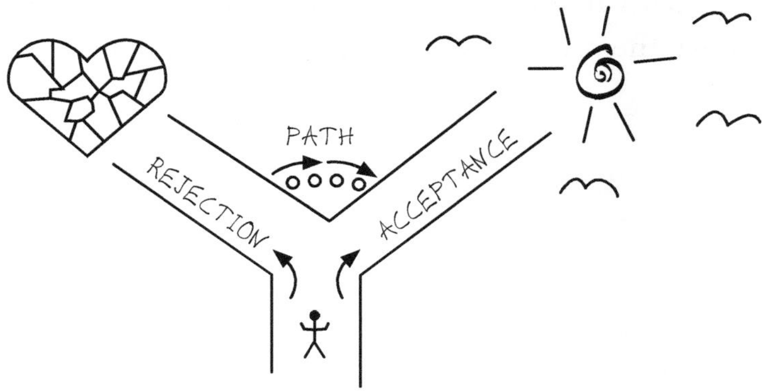

Steps to turn the mind

1. OBSERVE: Notice when I am angry or not accepting reality. Am I angry or bitter? Thinking "Why me?" or "This shouldn't be happening."
2. MAKE AN INNER COMMITMENT: Turn my mind from the rejection road to the acceptance road. Make the choice to accept. Imagine turning your mind and body to acceptance; walk the path from rejection over to acceptance any time!
3. DO IT AGAIN: You may have to do steps 1 and 2, over and over. That's okay!
4. PLANS: Develop a plan to think ahead, coping with future times of not accepting.

Adapted from Linehan, *DBT Skills Training Manual* (2015b)

~ Worksheet Directions ~

Review the concept of turning the mind. Alternatively, encourage a teen to review the steps aloud.

Also, remind the teens of the visual cues on the page:

> Turning the mind starts at a fork in the road, with a choice between accepting and rejecting reality. The fork in the road, drawn on the page, illustrates the two choices.
>
> Choosing the acceptance road has a positive outcome in life. Thus, the end of the acceptance road shows a doodle of a relaxing day of sunshine and birds.
>
> Choosing the rejection road ends poorly in life, as depicted by the image of a broken heart.
>
> In step 2, the teens make an inner commitment to turn to acceptance. On the worksheet, there is a rock pathway leading from the rejection road to the acceptance road. Teens can use this picture to imagine choosing this path at any point…they have a choice to leave the rejection road and move themselves over to the acceptance road.

Use the vignette below (this vignette is reflected in the completed worksheet), or pose another situation to the teens. As a group, discuss all four steps based on the vignette and Micah's experience. As additional practice, role-play the situation.

Vignette

Micah is 17 years old and will be a senior in high school. This summer, he's working as a lifeguard. After everyone leaves the pool at the end of the day, it's the lifeguards' responsibility to "clean and close up" the pool area.

Micah has noticed that several of the lifeguards are careless and don't close up according to pool staff rules. He has pointed this out to his peers on several occasions, and they just joke about Micah's "seriousness." Micah considers talking to the head lifeguard, Dan, but he doesn't want his friends to get mad at him.

One morning, Micah comes into work and sees a note to all the lifeguards, reprimanding them for not closing up the pool area properly. Dan mentions to Micah that he feels very let down and expects more from him. Micah tries to explain what has occurred over the past few weeks, but Dan is not interested and states: "Those are excuses. You've been here longer than most, and it's your responsibility to keep the pool up to expectations."

Micah feels very frustrated, and notices that he is having trouble accepting the reprimand. He continues to feel stuck in being mad and thinking, "I didn't do anything wrong."

Turning the Mind

dt

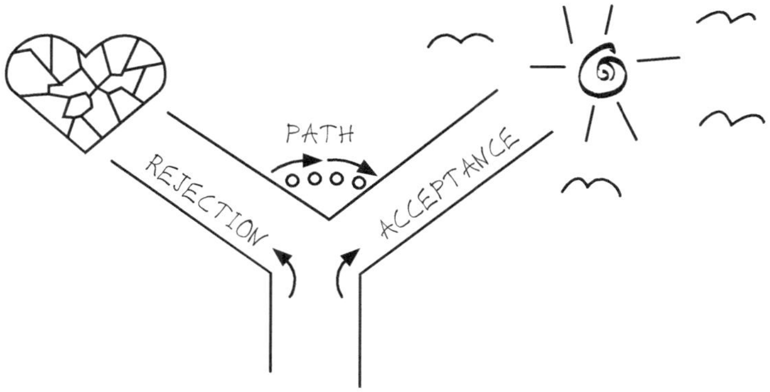

Steps

1. OBSERVE (notice not accepting): angry, frustrated, "It's not fair."
2. INNER COMMITMENT (accept reality): I can imagine turning my mind and body to accept Dan's comments and my leadership role.
3. DO IT AGAIN (keep taking the path over to acceptance): Every time I notice myself going back to feeling frustrated, I'll take a deep breath, and turn my mind and body to acceptance.
4. PLANS TO CATCH MYSELF (cope ahead): Next time I am corrected at work, I'll take a deep breath and think, "I can handle this calmly."

Adapted from Linehan, *DBT Skills Training Manual* (2015b)

Turning the Mind

dt

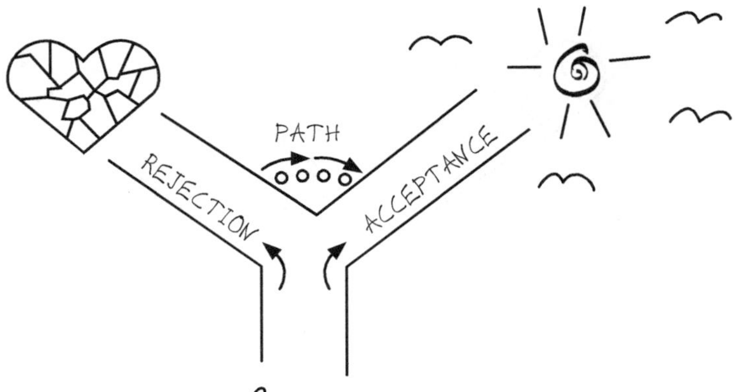

Steps

1. OBSERVE (notice not accepting):

2. INNER COMMITMENT (accept reality):

3. DO IT AGAIN (keep taking the path over to acceptance):

4. PLANS TO CATCH MYSELF (cope ahead):

Adapted from Linehan, *DBT Skills Training Manual* (2015b)

10. Reality Acceptance Skills: Radical Acceptance

Radical acceptance is a distress tolerance skill. The skill's name inherently describes its meaning: "radical" indicates total, full, and complete; and "acceptance" signifies an allowance and yielding to the reality of a situation.

Teens learn radical acceptance because life presents many unpleasant situations, facts, and emotions, and they have to learn to accept them. Rejecting or trying to change reality does not change it anyway. Remind the teens: radical acceptance does not mean that they like or agree with the situation, it only means that they will not get stuck in misery and in fighting against reality.

In the radical acceptance skill, teens will be learning two skills with two sets of handouts and worksheets. The first will discuss choices that teens can make to accept reality, and the second will outline steps to radical acceptance. The following vignette will be used to further illustrate both radical acceptance skills.

Vignette

Jean is a 15-year-old girl who lives with her mother, father, and two younger sisters—Isabel and Greta. In her DBT individual session, Jean complains that her parents' rules are "strict and unreasonable." She often gets into trouble for not following the rules, and she has actually gained more rules due to ignoring or trying to get around her family rules.

Jean is a bright girl and has always done well in school. Over the past year, however, Jean has made attempts to "show my parents their rules are overboard" by refusing to turn in her homework assignments. She nearly failed two classes last year due to numerous missing assignments.

10(a) Choices to accept reality

James J. Mazza *et al.*'s (2016) book, *DBT Skills in Schools*, describes four choices that teens can make as they work to accept reality:

1. Figure out how to solve the problem.
2. Change how you feel about the problem.
3. Accept the situation.
4. Stay miserable or make things worse by acting on impulsive urges.

Teens are encouraged to try first solving the problem and changing how they feel. If those two options are not available or possible, then teens are advised to accept the situation. If they are unable to accept the situation, then they remain stuck in misery until they are ready to do otherwise.

~ Handout Directions ~

Explain the Choices to Accept Reality skill to the teens. The first handout helps teens to understand their choices as they struggle to accept reality.

When faced with a problem, teens have four choices that they can make. The handout illustrates those four choices as well as questions that correspond to each choice:

1. First, they can attempt to solve the problem using wise options.
2. Second, they can change how they feel about a problem by viewing it in a new way: teens can say or think things to themselves to feel better about the situation, or they can use emotion regulation skills to find an emotional balance.
3. When choices 1 and 2 do not work, they need to move to accepting the problem. Of course, that does not mean that they like or agree with it. It merely indicates that they are accepting the situation as it is.
4. Finally, if they are unable to find an accepting space, they will remain in misery...stuck. If the teens act on their urges, it can become even worse, which surely ends in a more painful situation or outcome.

After explaining the handout, review it further with a vignette. The vignette can be the one above, one of yours, or it can be one suggested by the teens as an unpleasant problem that they have faced.

Read and encourage the teens to answer the questions that correspond to each choice.

Together, discuss the short- and long-term consequences of staying stuck in choice 4.

Choices to Accept Reality

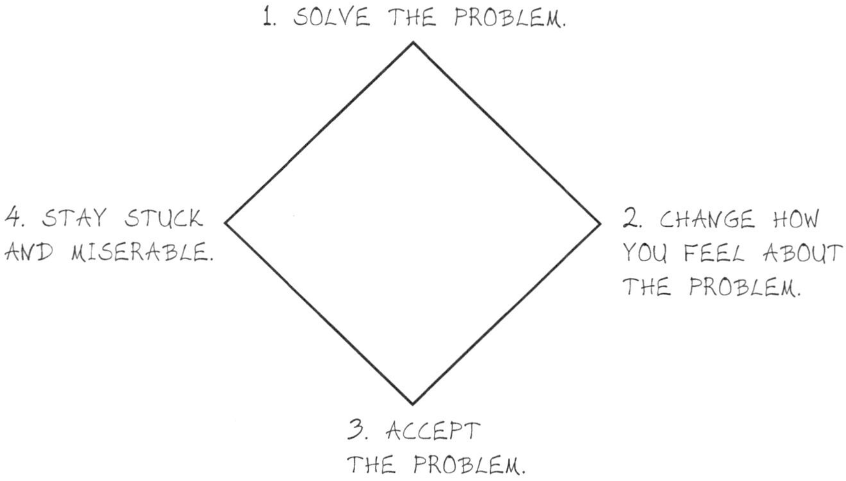

1. Can this problem be solved? What are some wise solutions? Can I avoid or get out of the situation?
2. What can I say to myself to feel better in the situation? Are there emotion regulation skills that I can use?
3. Can I tolerate or accept the problem? What reality acceptance statements can I say to myself?
4. Do I want to stay stuck and miserable? What are the short-term and long-term consequences of staying stuck?

Adapted from Mazza *et al.*, *DBT Skills in Schools: Skills Training for Emotional Problem Solving for Adolescents (DBT STEPS-A)* (2016)

~ Worksheet Directions ~

Review the choices to accept reality skill with the teens, or encourage one of them to review the skill aloud. The first worksheet guides teens to ponder situations they are facing or have faced in the past, and the choices they can make to accept reality.

Encourage them to use the questions on the handout to identify ways to solve the problem:

Choice 1: Solve the problem.

Choice 2: Change how they feel about the problem.

Choice 3: Accept the problem.

Choice 4: Stay stuck and miserable.

After explaining the worksheet, review it further with a vignette. The vignette can be one of yours or it could be one suggested by the teens as an unpleasant problem that they have faced.

Choices to Accept Reality

dt

The problem:
My parents' rules

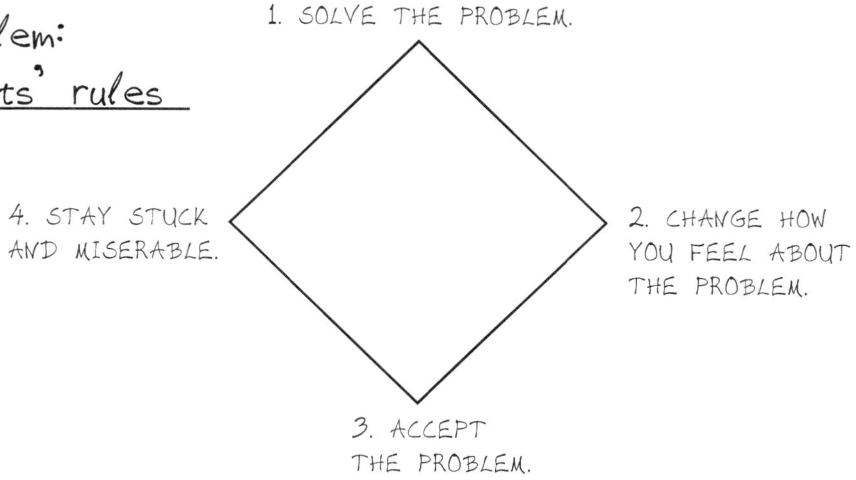

1. Follow the rules, turn in my homework.

2. Remind myself: my parents' rules are there to keep me safe. I can validate my feelings of frustration.

3. "I am accepting that I have rules—like all my friends."

4. Ugh! Consequences—more rules, fail a class, be home a lot.

Adapted from Mazza *et al.*, *DBT Skills in Schools: Skills Training for Emotional Problem Solving for Adolescents (DBT STEPS-A)* (2016)

Choices to Accept Reality

The problem:

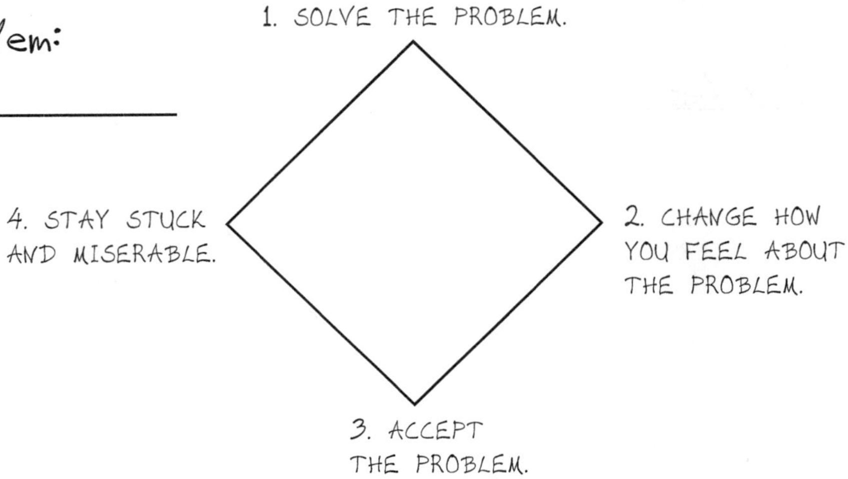

1.

2.

3.

4.

Adapted from Mazza *et al.*, *DBT Skills in Schools: Skills Training for Emotional Problem Solving for Adolescents (DBT STEPS-A)* (2016)

10(b) Radical Acceptance, Steps

Radical Acceptance is a distress tolerance skill. Following are steps to radical acceptance. The steps are adapted from Linehan's list in *DBT Skills Training Manual* (2015b):

1. Observe myself: my thoughts, feelings, body cues, words, and tone of voice. Observe any signs that I am questioning or fighting reality:
   "Am I questioning or fighting reality?"

2. Remind myself that this unpleasant reality "is what it is," and usually it cannot be changed.
   "It is what it is…"
   "It cannot be changed and I will accept it."

3. Consider causes of the reality. Sometimes, when you know the causes of the reality, it is easier to accept it. You may have to look at all the past causes to fully understand the current reality.

4. Practice fully accepting the reality. To allow acceptance to occur, you have to fully accept it with your mind, body, and spirit. They are all linked together. As an example, if you are not accepting in any area you may notice:
   Your mind might say, "It can't really be happening; I won't accept it."
   Your body and muscles may be tight. Practice relaxing them.
   Your spirit may be rejecting the reality.

5. Fully Engage in Practicing Opposite Action (distress tolerance skill). Some suggestions to accomplish this are:
   Act as though you accept the situation. Demonstrate acceptance with a calm voice, relaxed face (half-smile), open body posture (uncrossed arms and open hands), and words ("I accept this." "It is what it is.")
   Close your eyes, take some deep breaths, and imagine yourself accepting the situation.

6. Cope Ahead (emotion regulation skill). Identify any possible situations that may seem unacceptable.
   Imagine the situation and successfully accepting it.
   Practice accepting the situation with your body, mind, and spirit. (See step number 4.)

7. Allow your emotions. As you allow acceptance, you may notice feelings of sadness, disappointment, or grief, and that is okay! Even though feelings seem like facts, they are not.

   Practice Surfing the Wave (emotion regulation skill). Be mindful of your emotions without acting on them. Observe your emotions coming and going like a wave.

8. Recognize the truth. Life can be worth living even when it is painful.

   Remind yourself that everyone has some pain in life.

   Say to yourself, "I can get through this hard time."

   Be compassionate towards yourself. If that is difficult, first imagine how you would show compassion to a loved one. Then, do the same for yourself.

9. Do Pros and Cons (distress tolerance skill). Fill out a Pros and Cons sheet for accepting the challenging situation. Keep the sheet nearby and review it.

~ Worksheet Directions ~

Hand out a worksheet to each teen, pages 1 and 2. Review the radical acceptance skill and the list of nine steps. Take your time and thoroughly explain each step. As you discuss the steps, and where possible, encourage the teens to role-play the step. Use the group time to practice the skills with the teens: role-play, say the statements out loud, and imagine using the skill with a vignette.

Radical Acceptance

Steps (page 1)

1. Observe myself:

   Observe my thoughts, feelings, body cues, words.

   Ask myself, "Am I questioning or fighting reality?"

2. Remind myself that reality "is what it is," and usually cannot be changed.

3. Consider the causes of the reality.

   Think, "What has led up to this moment?"

4. Practice full acceptance of the reality:

   - Body: Scan my body, practice relaxing any areas of tenseness. Use TIP skills.
   - Mind: Change my thinking to acceptance. Think, "It is what it is."
   - Spirit: Practice meditation or prayer.

5. Engage in opposite action:

   - Act as though you fully accept the situation: calm voice, relaxed face, open hands.

Adapted from Linehan, *DBT Skills Training Manual* (2015b)

Radical Acceptance

dt

Steps (page 2)

6. Cope ahead: Name any future times that may seem unacceptable. Imagine the situation and fully accept it.

7. Allow your emotions: As you allow acceptance, you may notice feelings of sadness, disappointment, and grief: that's okay!

   Remember: even though feelings seem like facts, they are not! Practice Surfing the Wave—observe your emotions coming and going like a wave.

8. Recognize the truth: Life can be worth living even when it's painful.

   - Remind yourself: Everyone has some level of pain. (Remember you won't always see others' pain on social media.)
   - Say to yourself, "I can get through this hard time."
   - Be compassionate towards yourself.

   If that's too hard, imagine how you would show compassion to your best friend and then do the same for yourself.

9. Do Pros and Cons: Fill out a Pros and Cons sheet for accepting the situation. Keep the sheet nearby and review it.

Adapted from Linehan, *DBT Skills Training Manual* (2015b)

11. Reality Acceptance Skills: Half-Smiling

Half-smiling is a distress tolerance skill that accompanies the skill, willing hands, from willfulness vs. willingness. They both demonstrate reality acceptance with the teen's body. Additionally, the half-smile helps teens to increase control over their emotions.

The half-smile is a slight upturn of the corners of the lips while relaxing the face, neck, and shoulders. One way for teens to get a body sense of half-smiling is to gently hold a pencil in their mouth. It is not a big, fake or sarcastic grin… this would only cause irritation or incite arguments with others.

~ *Worksheet Directions* ~

Provide a worksheet for each teen. Explain the concept of the DBT distress tolerance, reality acceptance skill, "half-smiling." Teach them the steps as outlined on the worksheet and found in other sources. Next, alongside the teens, practice the half-smile.

In the second half of the worksheet, teens will find typical times when they can utilize this skill in daily life. These would be great vignettes to role-play as well.

Half-Smiling

Steps

1. Relax your face from the top of your head to your chin. If it's hard to do, try tensing your facial muscles, and then relaxing them.
2. Next, allow both corners of your lips to turn up slightly. Try to take on a peaceful, calm facial expression.

Practice half-smiling

1. When my feelings are hurt.
2. When I first awaken in the morning.
3. When my feelings are overwhelming.
4. When I have negative thoughts.
5. When I do not want to accept something.
6. In free moments during the day.
7. When I start to feel out of control or shut down.

Adapted from Linehan, *DBT Skills and Training Handouts and Worksheets* (2015a)

Section 4

Emotion Regulation

1. What is Emotion Regulation (ER)?

Often, teens must figure out how to manage unpleasant or painful feelings on their own. In the process, they can develop habits that land them on either end of the emotion continuum: shut down (ignore or push feelings away) or act out (let their emotions take charge and become reactive).

In this section on emotion regulation, handouts and worksheets will assist skills trainers to help teens know their emotions better, and to develop skills to deal with them. Teens will learn a few emotion regulation skills by Linehan (2015b) and several innovative skills from Moonshine's (2008) book, *Dialectical Behavior Therapy, Volume II: The Worksheets*.

Through the activity book's handouts and worksheets, teens will learn new ways in which to understand feelings and to manage their emotions with a more successful outcome. They will explore and identify feelings. They will learn skills to deal with emotions: ways to change their unwanted emotional reactions, and ways to decrease their vulnerability to falling into negative reactions.

Remember, all the handouts and worksheets in this section have the initials "er" on the page to signify that they belong in the "emotion regulation" set of skills. Again, where possible, use kinesthetic learning through role plays and body movement so as to emphasize the teen's learning of new skills.

~ Handout Directions ~

This handout is an introduction to the emotion regulation skills, and uses visual cues to enhance further learning of the concepts. The handout guides the adult leader in defining emotion regulation, and provides an introductory list of the emotion regulation skills that we will be learning and practicing in the activity manual. There is room at the bottom of the page to add more emotion regulation skills that you would like your teen to learn.

What is Emotion Regulation?

er

Knowing my emotions & Dealing with my emotions

- Exploring and knowing my emotions
- Surfing the Wave
- PLEASE

- ABC
- Opposite Action
- Lemonade

2. Exploring and Knowing My Emotions

Teens have a varied level of awareness of emotions, depending on their family life and history. Teens' awareness may range from being very attuned to their feelings to not being attuned at all.

The first step to improving a teen's ability to manage feelings is to develop an awareness and understanding of them. As teens practice to observe, describe, and identify emotions, they become more cognizant of their emotions and are less likely to be overwhelmed by them.

Let us look further at steps to observe and describe emotions:

1. Name the Emotion: What emotion are you working on?
2. Prompting Event: What event caused the emotion? What event happened right before the emotion?
3. Interpretation of Event: What are your thoughts or beliefs that go with this emotion?
4. Biological Changes: What do you notice in your body (feelings, body sensations, urges) that go with this emotion?
5. Expressions and Actions: What are the expressions (facial expression, body language) and actions (statements or comments, behavior) that go with this emotion?
6. Secondary Emotion: Did I have any emotion to experiencing my emotion in question number 1?

~ *Worksheet Directions* ~

Provide a worksheet for each teen. You may need to give them more than one worksheet as each scenario may evoke more than one emotion. Explain the steps to explore and know emotions: use the above information as well as other sources.

Next, choose a vignette, or allow the teens to share an event from their own life that caused a challenging emotion.

Using the vignette, go through each step in the worksheet. Inform the teens that they may identify more than one emotion in an experience. This is perfectly normal! In this case, instruct the teens to focus on one emotion at a time, and use one worksheet per emotion.

When going over a vignette with the group, encourage the teens to identify their own responses to each question. Remind them that each individual has their own unique response (body, mind, behavior) to emotions.

Attempt to go through the steps with several vignettes in order to explore as many different emotions as possible. For further examples, Linehan's (2015a) *DBT Skills Training Handouts and Worksheets* lists numerous responses to various emotions, including: anger, disgust, envy, fear, happiness, jealousy, love, sadness, shame, and guilt.

Vignette

Rosa is 16 years old. This year, Rosa and her family moved to a new town, and she started attending a new school. Rosa keeps in touch with her friends from back home; she feels like she's getting to know people at her new school and developing friendships.

At lunchtime, Rosa sits at the lunch table with her new friends. A few minutes after she begins to eat, she looks over to the next table and sees some girls laughing together. It reminds her of her old school and the close friendships that she had to leave behind. In that moment, Rosa really misses her friends.

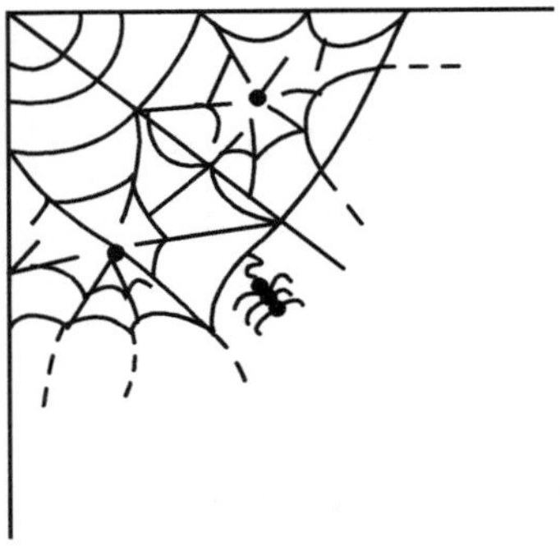

Exploring and Knowing My Emotions

1. Name of emotion ⟶

   Other words for the emotion: sadness, hurt, lonely, homesick.

2. What event caused the emotion? Seeing the other girls laughing and feeling closeness with friends...part of a group.

3. What are your thoughts or beliefs that go with the emotion?

   I don't have close friends.

   I'm alone.

4. What changes do you notice in your body (feelings, urges, body sensations)?

   Heaviness in my chest, on the verge of tears, an empty feeling.

5. What facial expressions or body language, and actions (comments, behavior) go with the emotion? Moping, withdrawing from lunch table, talking just a little bit, frowning.

6. What are your secondary emotions (the emotions about your emotion)? Embarrassed.

Adapted from Linehan, *DBT Skills and Training Handouts and Worksheets* (2015a)

er

Exploring and Knowing My Emotions

1. Name of emotion ⟶

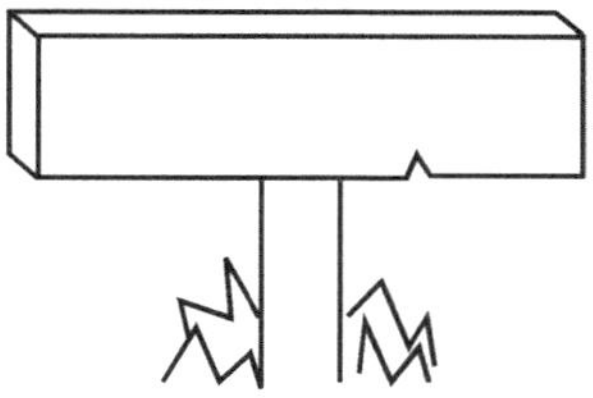

   Other words for the emotion:

2. What event caused the emotion?

3. What are your thoughts or beliefs that go with the emotion?

4. What changes do you notice in your body (feelings, urges, body sensations)?

5. What facial expressions or body language and actions (comments, behavior) go with the emotion?

6. What are your secondary emotions (the emotions about your emotion)?

Adapted from Linehan, *DBT Skills and Training Handouts and Worksheets* (2015a)

3. ABC

ABC is an emotion regulation skill and each letter stands for:

> A = Accumulate positive emotions, B = Build mastery, and C = Cope ahead.

ABC is a skill that helps teens reduce vulnerability to negative emotions, or helps them being in emotion mind. The ABC skill is usually taught with PLEASE skills, which address taking care of the body. Read about the PLEASE skills next in the emotion regulation section of the activity manual. Let's look further at each letter of the ABC skill:

> **A** = Accumulate positive emotions: as teens build a life worth living, they increase the pleasurable events in life. Pleasurable events are those that a teen can do in the moment (short term), such as: watching a favorite TV show or movie, building a model airplane, going on a hike, singing, and thinking about graduation. Long term, teens can think ahead to include more positive events in their life, and incorporate their goals and values. Some examples may include: doing a volunteer job to feel useful (Humane Society), having close relationships with family, being productive (at home and at school), and trying a new, exciting thing (zip lining).
>
> **B** = Build mastery: as teens build a feeling of mastery, they engage in activities that they enjoy and, additionally, that they find challenging. These activities will build a teen's sense of confidence, and also increase their feelings of competency. Some examples of build mastery include: working to get to first chair (the leader) in the orchestra when you are currently second chair, playing at a higher level of tennis (junior varsity team instead of freshman), lifting heavier weights at the gym, raising your GPA by a full point, and reading all the books in the *Harry Potter* series.
>
> **C** = Cope ahead: life continually changes and often throws unexpected (and expected) situations our way. Teens can develop a plan to manage feelings and problems that solve unexpected and expected challenges. For example, Janie has an upcoming class presentation. She is nervous about speaking in front of her peers, and she is worried that she will forget her speech. Alongside her teacher, Janie identifies ways to manage nervous feelings (deep breathing, validate her nervousness) and strategies in case she forgets her planned speech (glance at her note cards, practice it in front of her mom until she knows it well).

~ Handout Directions ~

Give a handout to each teen. Use the above information as well as other sources to explain the emotion regulation skill, ABC, to the teens. Remind the teens of the "er" icon in the upper-right corner, signifying that ABC belongs in the emotion regulation category of skills.

ABC

er

Accumulate positive emotions

- Increase pleasurable times in life:

  Short term (in the moment), such as: enjoying a sport or hobby

  Long term: Considering goals and values, such as: volunteering, having close relationships with family

Build mastery

· confident ·
· competent ·

- Engage in activities that build a feeling of confidence and competence that are a challenge. For example, raise my grade point average (GPA), get to the next level in a sport.

Cope ahead

Imagery

- Develop a plan to deal with expected and unexpected situations, i.e.: class speech
- Imagine the situation in the moment
- Imagine coping effectively

Adapted from Linehan, *DBT Skills Training Manual* (2015b)

~ Worksheet Directions ~

Give a worksheet to each teen, and review the emotion regulation skill, ABC.

In addition, provide an "Accumulate Positives Pleasant Activities List," found in Section 1, Skill 7(a). Teens will use this sheet to help them complete their individual accumulate positives list.

Once the teens have completed their worksheet, slowly go through each section. Encourage the teens to share their ideas with one another. Sharing ideas promotes further learning and brainstorming successful ways to use the ABC skill.

ABC

er

Accumulate positive emotions

SHORT TERM
- Get a manicure/pedicure
- Do a fun craft
- Pray
- Take the dog for a walk
- Watch a movie

LONG TERM
- Be a loyal friend
- Be honest
- Be responsible
- Work with homeless kids

Build mastery

- confident
- competent

- Get homework done—daily
- Clean my room—weekly
- Practice voice and guitar—30 minutes per day
- Increase weights at workout
- Walk 2 miles/day
- Learn to cook; start with salads

Cope ahead

Imagery

- Talk to teachers about extra credit
- Ask Mom about going to prom
- Finish whole song at next recital
- Score 15 points in basketball game

Adapted from Linehan, *DBT Skills Training Manual* (2015b)

ABC

er

Accumulate positive emotions

SHORT TERM

LONG TERM

Build mastery

- confident
- competent

Cope ahead

Imagery

Adapted from Linehan, *DBT Skills Training Manual* (2015b)

4. Surfing the Wave

As we deal with challenging emotions in life, it feels like they are going to last *forever*! So, not only are we dealing with the physical and emotional presence of the emotion, but we are also dealing with the thought, "I'm always going to feel like this..." This hopeless thought may be especially true for teens who have not experienced enough life to know that feelings are not facts and *emotions do not last forever*.

Painful emotions may arise from disappointing or difficult facts, situations, or people; or they may arise from painful feelings such as anxiety or depression. Emotions can be strong at times, and it may feel like they are going to knock us over; other times they are weak and as the emotional wave comes in we barely even notice it. Emotions rise and fall like waves in the ocean.

Teens must accept there will be times of difficult emotions, and they must learn to get through these to the other side. The DBT skill, "Surfing the Wave," helps teens to navigate through these painful times and let go of emotional suffering. Teens can learn to be mindful and aware of emotions without acting on them. Teens can learn to get through tough experiences, keep their balance and surf the wave. Assist teens to learn the following steps in understanding how to surf through waves of emotion:

1. Observe the emotion. Take some deep breaths and notice the emotion like a wave, coming and going. As the emotion comes in be open, and observe the feeling; do not try to get rid of it, ignore it, block the emotion or even try to keep it around.

2. Be mindful of your body. Breathe and notice any body sensations; scan your body from the top of your head to your toes. Where do you notice any tension? Or emotions? Allow yourself to experience the feelings in your body, and notice as they recede again.

3. Remember, you are not your emotion. As the emotion hits, remember you are not your emotion and it will not last forever. Take a deep breath and imagine creating a separation between yourself and your emotion; imagine a sturdy wall between yourself and the emotion. Remember and reflect on times in the past when you have felt differently.

4. Radically accept your emotions. Do not judge your emotions or yourself for having them. Practice radically accepting your emotions, and validate yourself:

"I can deal with these emotions and get through to the other side."

"I accept my sadness is here right now. I know I can handle it and it will go away again."

~ Handout Directions ~

Provide a handout for each teen. Teach them the emotion regulation skill, "Surfing the Wave," as described above and in other sources. Slowly go through each step, describing each one and demonstrating (i.e., deep breathing) where possible.

Surfing the Wave

1. Observe the emotion:
   - Notice the emotion like a wave, coming and going.
   - Do not try to get rid of it, ignore it, or try to make it bigger.
2. Be mindful of your body:
   - Scan your body from head to toe.
   - Notice any body sensations or emotions.
3. Remember, you are not your emotions:
   - Create a separation between yourself and your emotions.
   - Remember times when you have felt differently.
4. Radically accept your emotions:
   - Do not judge your emotions or yourself for having them.
   - Validate your emotions and say to yourself, "I can deal with these emotions and get through them."

Adapted from Linehan, *DBT Skills Training Manual* (2015b)

~ *Worksheet Directions* ~

Provide a worksheet for each teen. Review the emotion regulation skill, surfing the wave. Use the above information to describe the steps.

Alongside the teens, go through each step of a challenging event that they have faced or an event from the list below. Enlist the teens' help to discuss and role-play several situations in order to practice the steps.

Challenging events to discuss and role-play:

Your boyfriend/girlfriend tells you that he/she wants to break up.

A close family member is in the hospital.

You just found out that your parents are having some pretty serious marital problems.

You just heard that you didn't make the sports team/play/orchestra/other group at school.

You studied fairly hard for a test and just saw your grade...D.

Your favorite pet is old. When you left home this morning, he wasn't doing well.

You don't like being in school.

You failed the driving test today...for the third time.

Your parents don't approve of your boyfriend/girlfriend. You really like him/her.

Surfing the Wave

1. Observe the emotion. Observe and describe my emotions:
    - Am I blocking, ignoring, or trying to get rid of my emotions?
    - Am I holding onto emotions?
2. Be mindful of my body.
    - Scan my body; notice and describe any tension, body sensations, or emotions.
3. Remember, you are not your emotion.
    - Imagine a separation between myself and my feelings.
    - Name times I have felt differently:
4. Radically accept the emotion:
    - Am I judging myself?
    - Am I validating my emotions?
    - My validating statement:

Adapted from Linehan, *DBT Skills Training Manual* (2015b)

5. Opposite Action

Opposite Action, an emotion regulation skill, is useful for a teen to change or reduce their problematic emotions or behavior urges. Emotions can lead to behavior urges, and behavior urges can lead to emotions. Thus, by changing the emotion, the behavior urge can change; or by changing the behavior, the emotion can change. A few behavior urges that become problematic for a teen are: hitting, cursing, saying mean comments, isolating, and running away.

The following are steps to Opposite Action:

1. *Identify and name the emotion*: Name my problematic or unwanted emotion.
2. *Check the facts*: See if my emotion is justified by the facts of the situation. Does the emotion fit the facts of the situation? Does my wise mind say that the emotion, its intensity, and duration, fit the facts of the situation?
3. *Identify and describe my action urges*: What do I feel like saying or doing? Remember to pay attention to my facial expressions, tone of voice, and body language (teens may overlook them).
4. *Ask wise mind*: Is it effective for me to express this feeling or behavior? What is my goal? Will this lead to a positive or negative short-term or long-term outcome?
5. *Identify opposite actions to my behavior urge*: Identify the full opposite action to my behavior. At first, teens may have a hard time identifying the full opposite action. Initially, teens may say, "I shouldn't do the behavior; I need to stop," or they will choose an opposite action that is a slight change. It takes a few examples and repetitions for them to get the hang of it. As an example, when feeling afraid, approach the situation; and when angry, be a little nice and practice half-smiling.
6. *Act opposite to the urge*: Do the opposite…all the way.
7. *Repeat as needed*: I will continue to do the opposite action until my emotion changes.

~ Handout Directions ~

Give each of the teens a handout. Explain the emotion regulation skill, "Opposite Action," using the above information as well as other sources. Remind the teens that the "er" icon in the bottom-right corner of the worksheet indicates that opposite action falls into the emotion regulation group of skills.

Slowly go through the steps of the skill. Use a vignette to further demonstrate each step. Role-play the steps. Review several vignettes to give the teens more examples and a deeper understanding of the skill. It will take several examples until they understand how to identify a full (all-the-way) opposite action.

Opposite Action

1. Identify and name the problematic emotion:
2. Check the facts. See if the emotion, its duration and intensity, fits the facts of the situation.
3. Identify and describe the action urges:

   "What do I feel like doing or saying?"
4. Ask wise mind, "Is it effective for me to express this feeling or behavior?" Will this lead to positive or negative outcomes?
5. Identify opposite actions. Identify, *all* the way, the opposite action, i.e.:

   fear = approach, sad = be active.
6. Act opposite to the urge. Do it!
7. Repeat as needed. Continue until the emotion changes.

er

Adapted from Linehan, *DBT Skills Training Manual* (2015b)

~ Worksheet Directions ~

There are two worksheets available for this emotion regulation skill: one is a short form with more visual elements; and the other is a long form with more written instructions and less visual cues. Allow the teen to choose the worksheet best suited for their learning style. Of course, they may begin with one and then change to the other as time goes on. Whichever worksheet they pick is great, as long as their attitude is in a willing place to learn!

Review the steps with the teens or enlist a teen to review them for the group. Next, use a vignette to go through the steps to better illustrate using the skill. Verbally discuss and also role-play each step of the skill for deeper learning. It may take a few examples of fully turning to the opposite action for the teen to fully grasp the concept of opposite action. The long form will be presented first, followed by the short form.

The following vignette will be used to illustrate the worksheets in the activity manual.

Vignette

Patrick is a junior in high school. He's one of the youngest guys in his class, and often feels like he doesn't fit in even though he has a lot of friends. He was painfully shy as a younger kid. Patrick wants to invite someone to the upcoming school dance but he's hesitant to ask anyone. His friend, Tim, told him that several girls were questioning if he'd planned to go to the dance with a date. One of the girls, Mandie, told Tim she'd like to go to the dance with Patrick.

Opposite Action

Steps

1. Name the problematic emotion: also, nervous, worried, and scared.

   FEAR

2. Check the facts:
   - Does my emotion (intensity and duration) fit the facts of the situation? No—there's no threat to my health, life, or well-being.
3. Identify and describe my action urges:
   - What do I feel like saying or doing? "I'm not going to ask anyone."
   - What are the urges that show in my tone of voice, facial expression, body? Avoid eye contact, turn away from people, use a quiet voice.
4. Ask wise mind:
   - Is it effective for me to express the urge?—NO
   - What is my goal? Have fun with friends, build self-confidence.
   - Will this lead to a positive or negative outcome? Describe it. Negative—I'll feel less confident in myself and in dating.
5. Identify opposite actions (all the way):
   - Walk up to Mandie with good eye contact.
   - Talk to Mandie with a confident voice.
   - Go to the dance with Mandie.
6. Act opposite to the urge. Repeat as needed.

er

Adapted from Linehan, *DBT Skills Training Manual* (2015b)

Opposite Action

Steps

1. Name the problematic emotion:

2. Check the facts:
    - Does my emotion (intensity and duration) fit the facts of the situation?

3. Identify and describe my action urges:
    - What do I feel like saying or doing?
    - What are the urges that show in my tone of voice, facial expression, body?

4. Ask wise mind:
    - Is it effective for me to express the urge?
    - What is my goal?
    - Will this lead to a positive or negative outcome? Describe it.

5. Identify opposite actions (all the way):
    -
    -
    -

6. Act opposite to the urge. Repeat as needed.

Adapted from Linehan, *DBT Skills Training Manual* (2015b)

Opposite Action

Steps

er

1. Name the problematic emotion:

   FEAR

2. CHECK:
   - Does it fit the facts? No.
   - Is it effective? Not at all... My goal is to have fun and learn dating.

3. Identify action urges:
   - Avoid the dance.
   - Not ask anyone to go.
   - Avoid eye contact, turn away when asking Mandie to go.

4. Identify opposite actions...all the way!

   180°

   - Walk up to Mandie with eye contact.
   - Talk to Mandie with a confident voice.
   - Go to the dance with Mandie.
   - Have fun at the dance!

5. Act opposite to your urge. Do it!
6. Repeat until the urge changes.

Adapted from Linehan, *DBT Skills Training Manual* (2015b)

Opposite Action

Steps

er

1. Name the problematic emotion:

2. CHECK:
   - Does it fit the facts?
   - Is it effective?

3. Identify action urges:

180°

4. Identify opposite actions...all the way!

5. Act opposite to your urge. Do it!

6. Repeat until the urge changes.

Adapted from Linehan, *DBT Skills Training Manual* (2015b)

6. PLEASE

PLEASE is an emotion regulation skill, and encourages teens to take care of their body. It is commonly known that the body and mind are well connected, and that one influences the other. It is difficult for anyone to keep their emotions regulated when their body is out of balance. When a teen takes consistent care of their body, their emotions are being taken care of as well, and they are less vulnerable to negative emotions.

PLEASE is an acronym. Let's look at each letter and its meaning:

1. Treat **P**hysica**l** Illness: Inform the teens to go to the doctor, take their prescribed medicine, and take it easy when they are sick. When people are ill, they are less likely to be in charge of their emotions and are more easily dysregulated. And missing medicine, especially psychiatric medicine, can cause havoc on a person's mood.

2. Balance **E**ating: Healthy foods and appropriate amounts of food are best for a teen's growing body. When a teen is hungry from not eating or from not eating nourishing foods, they are more likely to become dysregulated and stuck in negative emotions. A person needs to eat every 2–3 hours; three healthy meals and two healthy snacks.

3. Avoid Mood-**A**ltering Substances: Alcohol, drugs, and cigarettes make anyone more prone to dysregulation. The best advice: Stay away from alcohol, drugs, and cigarettes.

4. Balance **S**leep: Every teen needs the proper amount of sleep in order for their body and emotions to function well. Typically, most teens need either 7, 8, or 9 hours of sleep per night so as to maintain emotional balance during the day. It helps to develop a nightly sleep routine.

5. Get **E**xercise: Consistent exercise helps to maintain a balanced mood. Of course, it also helps a teen's body to function well. Encourage teens to find fun ways to exercise and set a goal for at least 20 minutes, 5–7 days per week.

Note: The handout and worksheet look fairly similar at a distance. In order to differentiate the two, the PLEASE Skills heading background is shaded on the worksheet and left white on the handout.

~ Handout Directions ~

Give a handout to each teen. Explain the PLEASE skill from the above information and other sources. Discuss each letter on the handout, its meaning, and a description of the skill.

You may also provide the coordinating handout, "Sleep Tight—Suggestions for Better Sleep," found in Section 1, Skill 7(d). This handout coordinates with the letter "S" of the PLEASE skill, and stands for "Balance Sleep." The handout offers eight ideas for teens to improve their sleep habits.

PLEASE Skills

1.
Treat
Physical Illness:
- Go to the doctor, as needed.
- Take your prescription (Rx) medicine.
- Take it easy when you're ill.

2. Balance Eating:
- Eat nourishing foods.
- Eat appropriate amounts of food.

er

3. Avoid Mood-Altering Substances:
- Alcohol and drugs make you prone to negative emotions.
- Stay away from alcohol and drugs.

4. Balance Sleep:
- Your body needs the appropriate amount of sleep in order to regulate emotions.
- Most teens need 7, 8, or 9 hours every night.

5. Get Exercise:
- Consistent exercise maintains a balanced mood.
- Have a goal of 20 minutes, 5-7 days a week.

Adapted from Linehan, *DBT Skills Training Manual* (2015b)

~ Worksheet Directions ~

Give a worksheet to each teen. Remember, the worksheet has the PLEASE Skills heading background shaded to distinguish it from the handout. Review the letters of the acronym, PLEASE, or ask a teen to review the emotion regulation skill.

Also, review the coordinating handout, "Sleep Tight—Suggestions for Better Sleep," found in Section 1, Skill 7(d). This handout coordinates with the letter "S" for "Balance Sleep," and offers eight ideas for teens to improve their sleep habits.

This worksheet can be discussed individually or as a group. Read the questions aloud under each letter category.

Discuss the questions as a group. Some potential questions to ask are:

> Identify ways to say, "No," and to keep boundaries with others who use substances.
>
> What are some of the ideas from the "Sleep Tight" handout that I am willing to try?
>
> What are some fun ways to exercise that I'd be willing to try?

If possible, role-play setting boundaries with peers who offer the teen alcohol, drugs, or cigarettes. Ask, "How can your face, body language, tone of voice, and words set a firm limit with your peer?"

PLEASE Skills

1. Treat Physical Illness:

- Do I need to see the doctor? No.
- Am I consistently taking my Rx medicine? Yes!

2. Balance Eating:

- Am I eating nourishing foods? Mostly.
- Am I eating appropriate portions of food? Nope, need to work on it.

er

3. Avoid Mood-Altering Substances:

- Am I staying away from alcohol and drugs? Yes!
- Identify ways to say, "No," and to keep boundaries with others who use substances: Don't hang out with people who use substances.

4. Balance Sleep:

- How much sleep does my body need (nightly) to function well? 9 hours
- Which ideas can I try from the "Sleep Tight" handout? Go to sleep at the same time every night.

5. Get Exercise:

- What are some fun ways to exercise that I'd be willing to try? Bike-riding, trampoline, walking.

Adapted from Linehan, *DBT Skills Training Manual* (2015b)

PLEASE Skills

1\. Treat **P**hysical I**l**lness:

- Do I need to see the doctor?
- Am I consistently taking my Rx medicine?

2\. Balance **E**ating:

- Am I eating nourishing foods?
- Am I eating appropriate portions of food?

er

3\. Avoid Mood-**A**ltering Substances:

- Am I staying away from alcohol and drugs?
- Identify ways to say, "No," and to keep boundaries with others who use substances:

4\. Balance **S**leep:

- How much sleep does my body need (nightly) to function well?
- Which ideas can I try from the "Sleep Tight" handout?

5\. Get **E**xercise:

- What are some fun ways to exercise that I'd be willing to try?

Adapted from Linehan, *DBT Skills Training Manual* (2015b)

7. Lemonade

"Lemonade" is an emotion regulation skill discussed by Moonshine (2008). In cognitive behavior therapy, this concept is referred to as a "cognitive reframe," and is a way in which to see negative events, feelings, or thoughts from a new or different perspective.

Lemonade skill helps the teen to take a belief, and turn it from a weakness into a strength. It allows the teen to see the bigger picture of a feeling, situation, or belief. Moonshine mentions that one example is to see life problems and its emotional pain as an opportunity to practice DBT skills.

I would like to add a couple of steps to practice lemonade:

1. Take an irrational or negative thought, and change the wording to incorporate more positive, gentle words. Make a comment without judgment; stick with the facts. For example, instead of saying, "I'm so stupid. I can't learn this math!" change it to, "I'm learning this math. Everyday I'm getting better. It's taking longer and is a lot more frustrating than I thought it would be!"

2. Ask, "What can I learn from this situation?" Look for the blessing or silver lining. Let's look at the example of Annie, who is a college sophomore.

Annie's parents give her money for rent and other expenses. Each month, she is in charge of paying the utility bill for herself and her roommates. In the month of November, Annie spent all the money from her mom, plus all of the utility money from her roommates. Finally, broke and emotionally broken, Annie confesses her poor decision to her mom—she did not have enough money to pay the upcoming utility bill. Annie's mom pays the bill and, as a consequence, Annie has to forfeit all but one of her soon-to-be Christmas gifts.

At first, Annie is humiliated and devastated. Then, she asks herself, "What can I learn from this situation?" Annie is able to name numerous ways in which she has learned from the experience, including: a felt sense of trust with her mom, finally being open and willing to learn better ways of managing money, and an increased sense of maturity.

~ *Worksheet Directions* ~

Provide a worksheet for each teen. Teach them the lemonade skill, and describe the steps. As a group, discuss some vignettes or true-life situations that they may face. Verbally rehearse and then role-play, using the lemonade skill. Some possible vignettes are:

> Your boyfriend/girlfriend tells you that he/she wants to break up.
>
> You just heard that you didn't make the sports team/play/orchestra/other group at school.
>
> You studied fairly hard for a test and just saw your grade…D.
>
> You failed the driving test today…for the third time.

lemonade

1. Change the wording; use gentler words and facts.

FROM:

"I'm an idiot!"

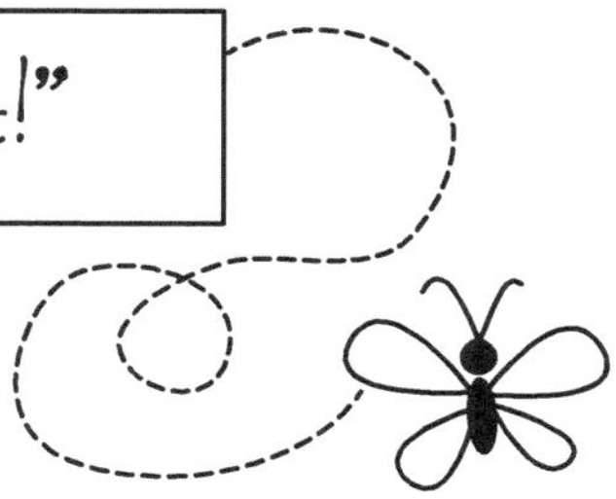

TO:

"I'm sad that I spent money I didn't have."

2. Ask, "What can I learn from this situation?"

- I know that I can turn to Mom for help.
- I'm ready to learn how to budget money.
- I'm learning and maturing.

lemonade

1. Change the wording; use gentler words and facts.

FROM:

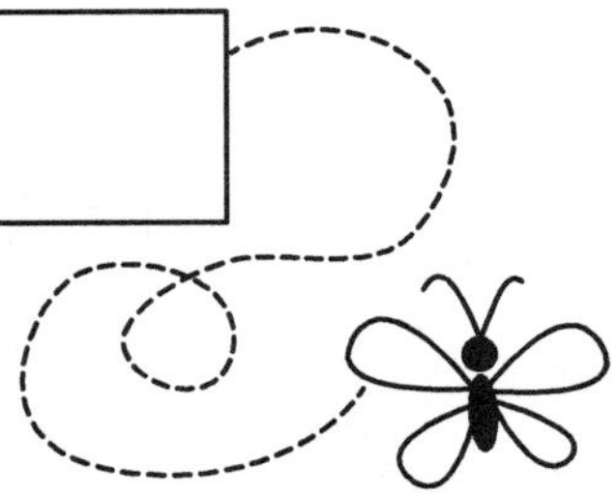

TO:

2. Ask, "What can I learn from this situation?"

Section 5

Interpersonal Effectiveness

1. What is Interpersonal Effectiveness (IE)?

Interpersonal effectiveness is the final set of DBT skills in the activity manual. The interpersonal effectiveness skills, developed by Linehan (2015b), address the teen being able to get needs met, maintain relationships, and have self-respect within relationships.

The activity manual will focus on some traditional skills from Linehan (2015b), including: GIVE and FAST. The activity manual includes several innovative interpersonal effectiveness skills from Moonshine (2008): Repairs and The Four Horsemen. Another skill, THINK, is also included in this section. Lastly, I have added an additional skill, TAPS. It is a skill for teens to give and receive emotional support in relationships.

~ *Handout Directions* ~

The handout guides the skills trainer in defining interpersonal effectiveness. It also provides an introductory list of skills that we will be learning and practicing in the activity manual. There is room at the bottom of the page to add additional skills.

Provide a handout for each of the teens. Explain that our next set of DBT skills is called "interpersonal effectiveness." Define and discuss "interpersonal effectiveness." Identify the new group of skills the teens will be learning: repairs, TAPS, THINK, The Four Horsemen, GIVE, and FAST.

What is Interpersonal Effectiveness?

1. Get your needs met.
2. Maintain relationships.
3. Have self-respect.

- Repairs
- The Four Horsemen
- TAPS
- GIVE
- THINK
- FAST

ie

2. Repairs

Repairs is an interpersonal effectiveness skill mentioned by Moonshine (2008). Moonshine included this skill to help teens have long-lasting, healthy relationships.

Repairs are necessary for relationships to heal from any mistakes or wrongdoing. This is especially true for teens as the nature of being a teen is to make mistakes, learn, and grow from them, and change into a healthy adult. The only way for this process to work is to make some mistakes! Keeping that in mind, I would like to add some steps to guide teens in learning the process of repairing breaks, or apologizing, in relationships:

1. *Address the person by name*: Addressing the person by name shows respect, and that you are taking the process seriously.
2. *Take responsibility*: Say specifically what you have done wrong as you begin your apology. Say, "I am sorry for _________." Remember, you are being specific. For example, "I am sorry for breaking your clock by trying to take it apart."
3. *Ask for forgiveness*: Say, "Can you forgive me?"
4. *Accept their answer with validation (and without arguing)*: At this point, the individual may accept your apology or they may not be quite ready to do so. If they are not ready, listen and validate their feelings or concerns. Show good eye contact, turn your body towards them, and validate their statements or feelings.
5. *Do things differently*: The person needs to know that the apology was heartfelt and sincere. The best way to show this is to behave in a new way. If you continue to make the same mistake, other people will believe that you are insincere and they may be reticent to accept additional apologies for the same behavior.

~ Handout Directions ~

Provide a handout for each teen, and teach the repairs skill and its steps. Read the steps and discuss the questions in each step.

Read a vignette or ask a teen to provide an example of a mistake or wrongdoing from their life. Next, using the vignette or example, go through each step and answer the questions in order to further illustrate using the repairs skill.

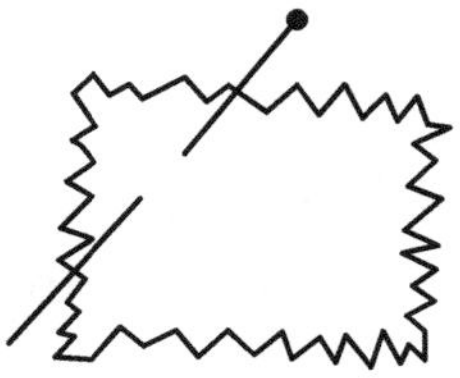

Repairs

1. **Address the person by name:** Show the person respect and that you are taking the situation seriously.

2. **Take responsibility:** Admit to your mistake or wrongdoing—be specific.

3. **Ask for forgiveness:** "Can you forgive me?"

4. **Accept their answer with validation:** "I understand..."

5. **Do things differently:** Behave in a new way that shows that your apology was sincere.

~ Worksheet Directions ~

Provide a worksheet for each teen. Ask the teens to offer an example of wrongdoing or a mistake from their own life to practice the repairs skill.

Instruct the teens to use their example to write a letter of apology to the person they hurt. They will follow the steps to write their letter.

After the letter is written, teens will role-play, saying their apology aloud. In life, they can choose to deliver their apology verbally or in writing.

Repairs

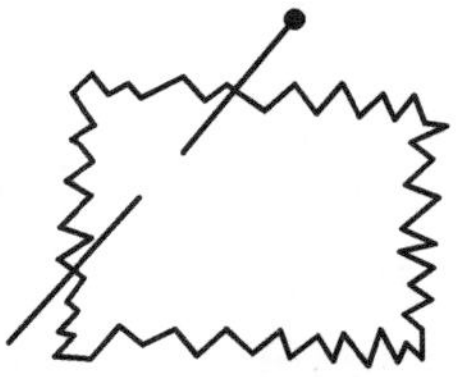

1. Address the person by name.
2. Take responsibility.
3. Ask for forgiveness.
4. Accept their answer with validation.
5. Do things differently.

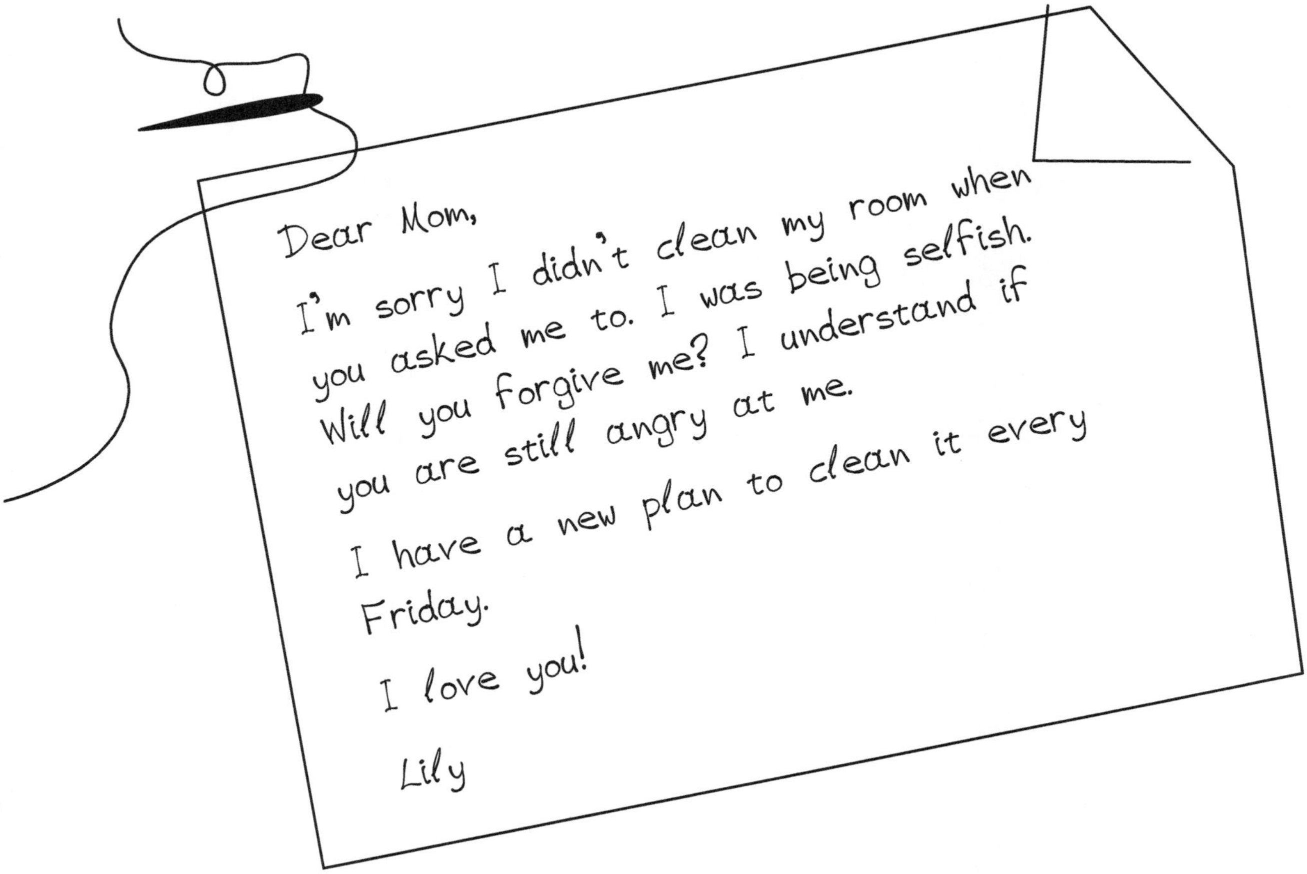

Dear Mom,

I'm sorry I didn't clean my room when you asked me to. I was being selfish. Will you forgive me? I understand if you are still angry at me.

I have a new plan to clean it every Friday.

I love you!

Lily

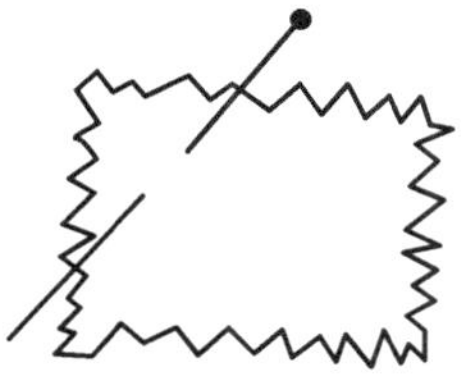

Repairs

1. Address the person by name.
2. Take responsibility.
3. Ask for forgiveness.
4. Accept their answer with validation.
5. Do things differently.

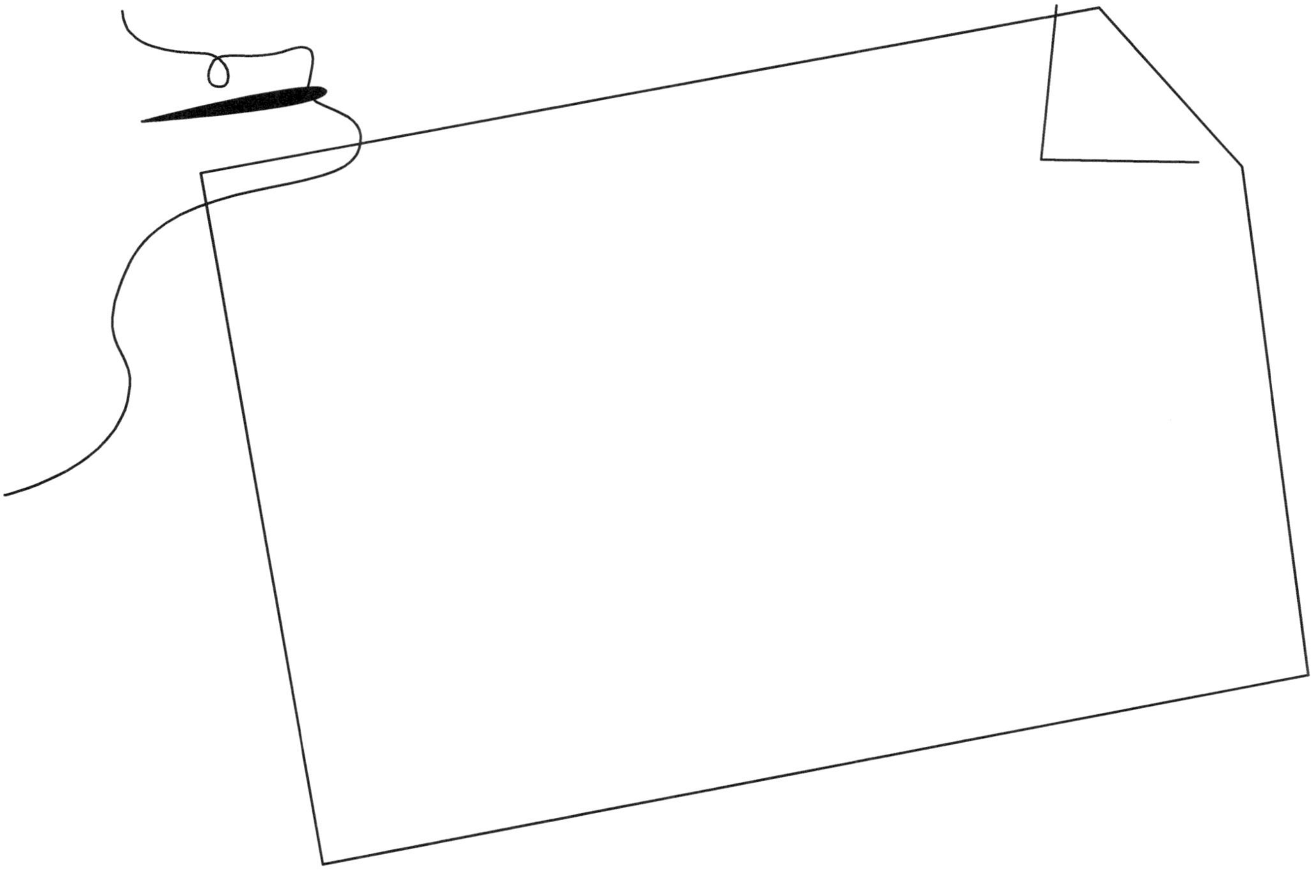

3. TAPS

TAPS, a new interpersonal effectiveness skill, teaches teens about the reciprocal nature of giving and receiving emotional support with others, including family, friends, and other caring adults. Teens need to be able to give and receive emotional support, and this skill is necessary and tricky during adolescence.

Developmentally, teens are at a stage of seeking independence, and it may feel counterintuitive to request or offer support with others. Furthermore, teens may shy away from asking for reassurance due to feelings of vulnerability, and choosing trustworthy people makes this task less arduous. On the flip side, teens need quite a bit of guidance as they wade through adolescent emotions, and social and relational situations that they have seldom navigated before.

When teens are able to ask for or offer help and comfort to emotionally safe people, it can be life changing. Life is easier when others walk alongside us during the peaks and valleys of life.

TAPS is an acronym and the letters stand for:

T = **T**alk to someone safe

A = **A**sk for reassurance

P = **P**ray or meditate

S = **S**eek support.

Let's look more closely at each letter and its meaning:

T = Talk to an emotionally safe person. Seek someone who has shown a pattern over time of loyal and trustworthy behavior; people whose words and behaviors match. Choose to share feelings within emotionally safe relationships so that you can share your feelings and concerns without judgment.

When offering help, be an emotionally safe person. Validate the person to whom you are speaking: maintain eye contact, listen without interrupting, face your body to theirs, and put all other distractions aside.

A = Ask for reassurance. In a healthy relationship, it is okay to ask for or offer reassurance. As you ask for reassurance, say, "What I need is…" or ask for appropriate, comforting touch, "Can I have a hug?" Be careful not to tip to the other side and become clingy: do not repeatedly ask for reassurance or comforting touch from someone.

As the one offering reassurance or appropriate touch, ask, "How can I help you?" or "Can I give you a hug?" Always ask first; it shows respect and healthy boundaries. Remember, agreeing to reassure another does not mean that you do whatever they are asking if it crosses a boundary line or requires you to give in to coercive or bullying behavior.

P = Pray or meditate. We all have times when we feel emotionally burdened or alone. When you feel alone, pray or seek support from God or your higher power. Offer to pray with or for another person; meditate together. Mindful meditation helps teens to be able to handle the moment and the situation without focusing on the past or future.

S = Seek support. Surround yourself by an emotionally safe community of friends, family, and caring adults whom you can turn to for emotional support. Presently, if you do not have a community, find a trusted therapist or therapy animal (dog, cat, bird) to provide healthy support until you build a trusted community.

~ Handout Directions ~

Provide a handout for each teen. Discuss the TAPS skill. Teach the teens each letter in the skill, and its meaning from the above information. As you discuss each letter, brainstorm ways to accomplish each task; for example, ask, "What are loyal and trustworthy behaviors?" or "What does it mean that a person's behavior and words match?" Role-play the steps for further practice.

TAPS ...giving and receiving

ie emotional support

1. **T** = Talk to an emotionally safe person. Someone with a pattern of loyal and trustworthy behavior, so that you can feel safe to share feelings.

2. **A** = Ask for reassurance, "What I need is..." or "Can I have a hug?" Be careful not to tip to repeated requests. Offer reassurance, "How can I help you?" or "Can I give you a hug?"

3. **P** = Pray or meditate when you are alone or in distress. Seek support from God or your higher power. Practice mindful meditation. Pray with a friend.

4. **S** = Seek support from a community, or find a trusted therapist, or therapy animal (dog, cat) until you build a community.

~ Worksheet Directions ~

Provide a worksheet for each teen. Review the TAPS skill, or enlist a teen to review the skill. After reviewing the skill, discuss the questions given with each letter of the skill.

Encourage the teens to share their completed worksheet or answers with one another.

TAPS ...*giving and receiving emotional support*

ie

1. **T** = · Has this person shown a pattern of safe behavior and words?

   · Can I share feelings without fear of criticism?

   · loyal
   · trustworthy

2. **A** =

· Ask for reassurance: "What I need is..." "Can I have a hug?" (Be careful not to tip to neediness.)

· Offer reassurance: "How can I help you?"

3. **P** = When I feel alone or in distress, I will: pray or meditate.
   My prayer or meditation:

4. **S** = My community is:

   If I don't have a community, I will talk to the therapist:
   or my therapy animal:
   until I build a community.

4. THINK

"THINK" is not a traditional or innovative DBT skill, rather it is a quote popularized by British author, pastor, and evangelist, Alan Redpath. I have included this skill because it encourages positivity in relationships. It helps relationships to bloom! The acronym guides teens in the way in which they speak, and in the words they choose to say with and about one another. For this skill, when teens say or even consider saying back talk, gossip, disrespectful comments, or hurtful words, we will refer to it as "word errors."

Instruct your teens to think before they speak, and to ask themselves, "Are my words true, helpful, inspiring, necessary, and kind?" Following are each letter and its meaning:

True: Speak the truth. Do not lie or exaggerate about yourself, others, or the facts.

Helpful: Be certain that your words are helpful and will bring aid to yourself or others. Will my words help or hurt myself or others? Will my words harm another person's feelings or self-esteem? If so, they are certainly not helpful.

Inspiring: Will your words be an inspiration? Make sure that your words will lift you or someone else up instead of tearing others down through criticism (verbal attacks) or disrespect (sarcasm, name-calling, eye-rolling, or mocking).

Necessary: Are your words *needed* or do you *want* to say them? Will they hurt, be vengeful, or create drama? If the teens' comments are not necessary, then it is important for them to remain silent. I grew up with the adage, "If you don't have something nice to say, then don't say it at all." It is a good rule to follow in keeping and maintaining relationships.

Kind: Are your words kind? Kindness brings people together, and forms healthy, loving relationships.

~ Handout Directions ~

Provide a handout for each teen. Teach them the acronym, THINK, describing and illustrating each letter of the word. Also, discuss short- and long-term consequences when teens use "word errors" in relationships in their life, including: peers, family, teachers, youth pastor, and coaches.

As a group, use vignettes to help illustrate noticing word errors and, instead, change comments to THINK words. Some possible vignettes include:

> One of your friends is wearing a really unattractive outfit or shirt.
>
> You saw one of the varsity sports players walk out of detention room.
>
> You overheard a teacher telling another student that they had failed a test.
>
> Your best friend and her boyfriend broke up because he cheated on her with a girl whom you do not like.

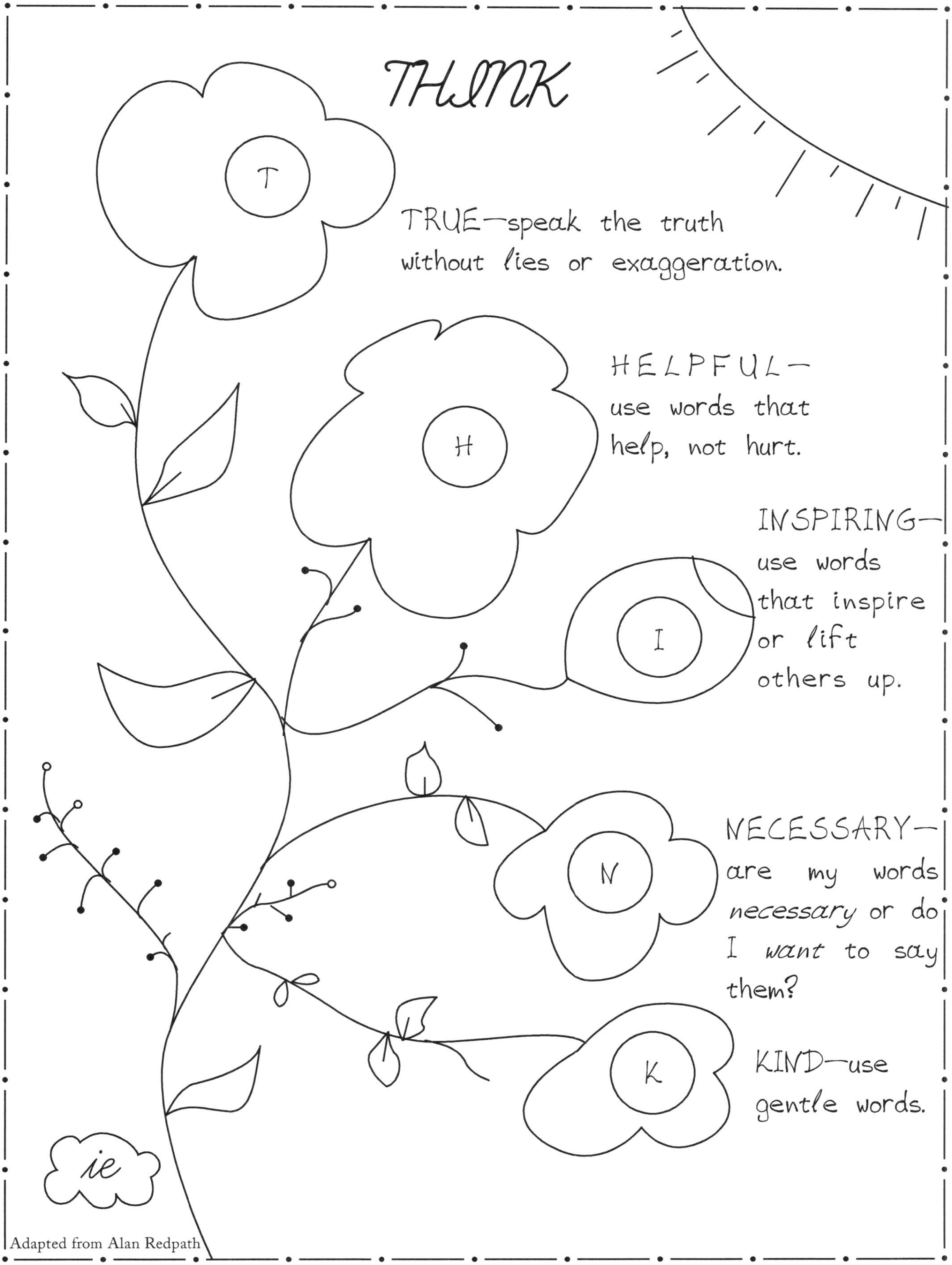
THINK
T
TRUE—speak the truth without lies or exaggeration.
H
HELPFUL—use words that help, not hurt.
I
INSPIRING—use words that inspire or lift others up.
N
NECESSARY—are my words *necessary* or do I *want* to say them?
K
KIND—use gentle words.
ie
Adapted from Alan Redpath

~ Worksheet Directions ~

Give a worksheet to each teen. Review the THINK skill with them. Encourage the teens to offer situations from their own lives to further discuss and review the skill. Remind the teen of short- and long-term consequences that arise from using hurtful words or "word errors."

On the worksheet, teens will choose a situation from their own life or a vignette to practice the THINK skill. As they use the skill, encourage them to notice and write down their "word errors." Next, teens will change their word errors to comments using the THINK skill.

Provide additional situations that the teens can discuss or role-play within the group to practice the skill. Some example vignettes are:

> One of your friends is wearing a really unattractive outfit or shirt.
>
> You saw one of the varsity basketball players walk out of the detention room.
>
> You overheard a teacher telling another student that they had failed a test.
>
> Your best friend and her boyfriend broke up because he cheated on her with a girl whom you do not like.

Vignette

For the completed worksheet, we will use the following vignette: Grace is 13 years old. She is close friends with Marci, who is dating Rich. Marci and Rich have been dating since 6th grade. Rich is a respectful boyfriend, and has always been very attentive and kind to Marci.

Grace is in the office waiting to call her mom because her stomach hurts. As Grace is waiting, she overhears two girls talking about Rich cheating on his girlfriend.

Grace quickly leaves the office to find Marci. She immediately thinks, "I need to find Marci so she can confront that jerk!"

SITUATION: MARCI

THINK

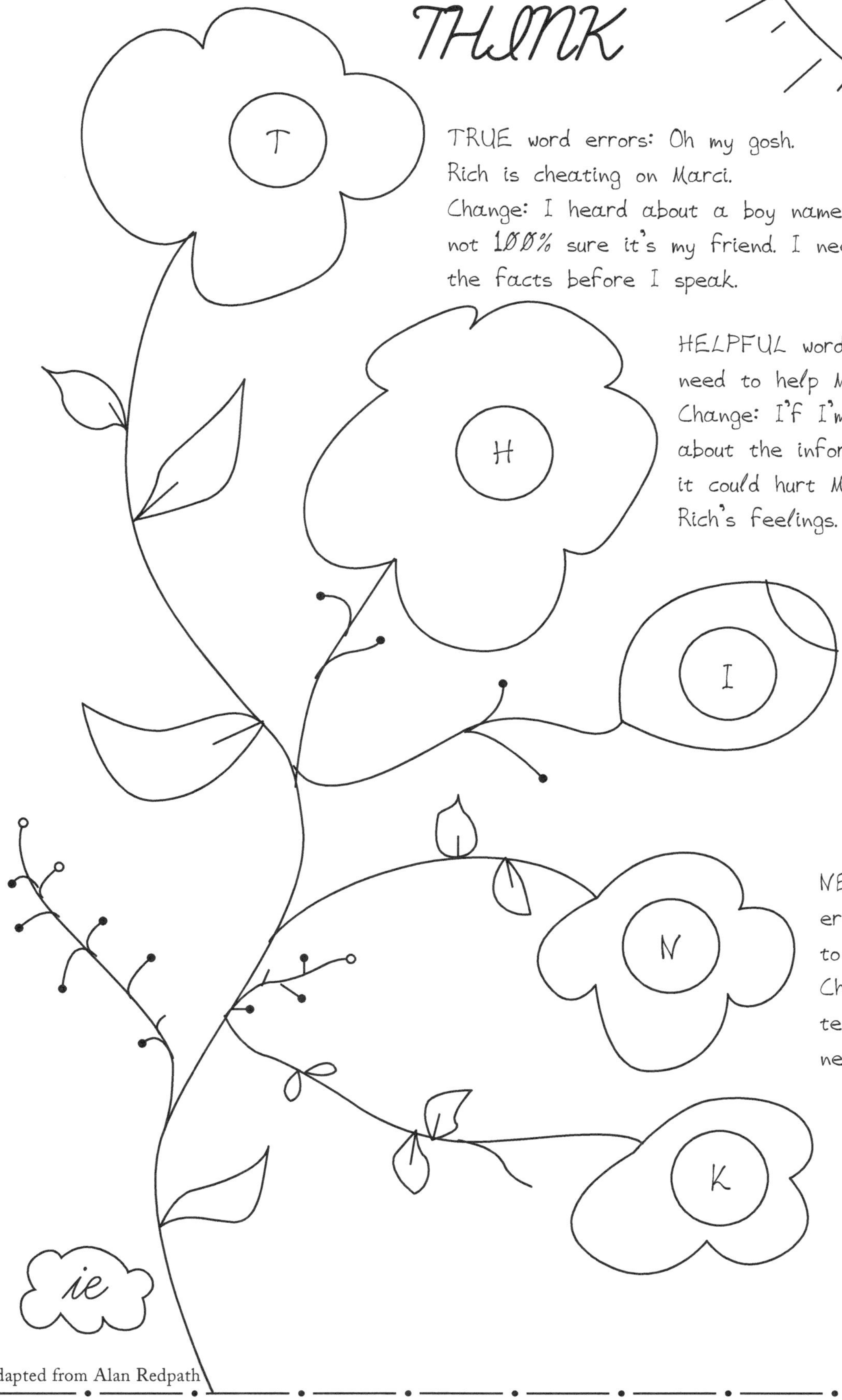

TRUE word errors: Oh my gosh. Rich is cheating on Marci.
Change: I heard about a boy named Rich. I'm not 100% sure it's my friend. I need to check the facts before I speak.

HELPFUL word errors: I need to help Marci.
Change: If I'm wrong about the information, it could hurt Marci and Rich's feelings.

INSPIRING word errors: It will help her to know.
Change: This will tear them down if it's not accurate.

NECESSARY word errors: Marci needs to know.
Change: I *want* to tell her; it's not necessary to gossip.

KIND word errors: That jerk!
Change: I'm mad at Rich.

Adapted from Alan Redpath

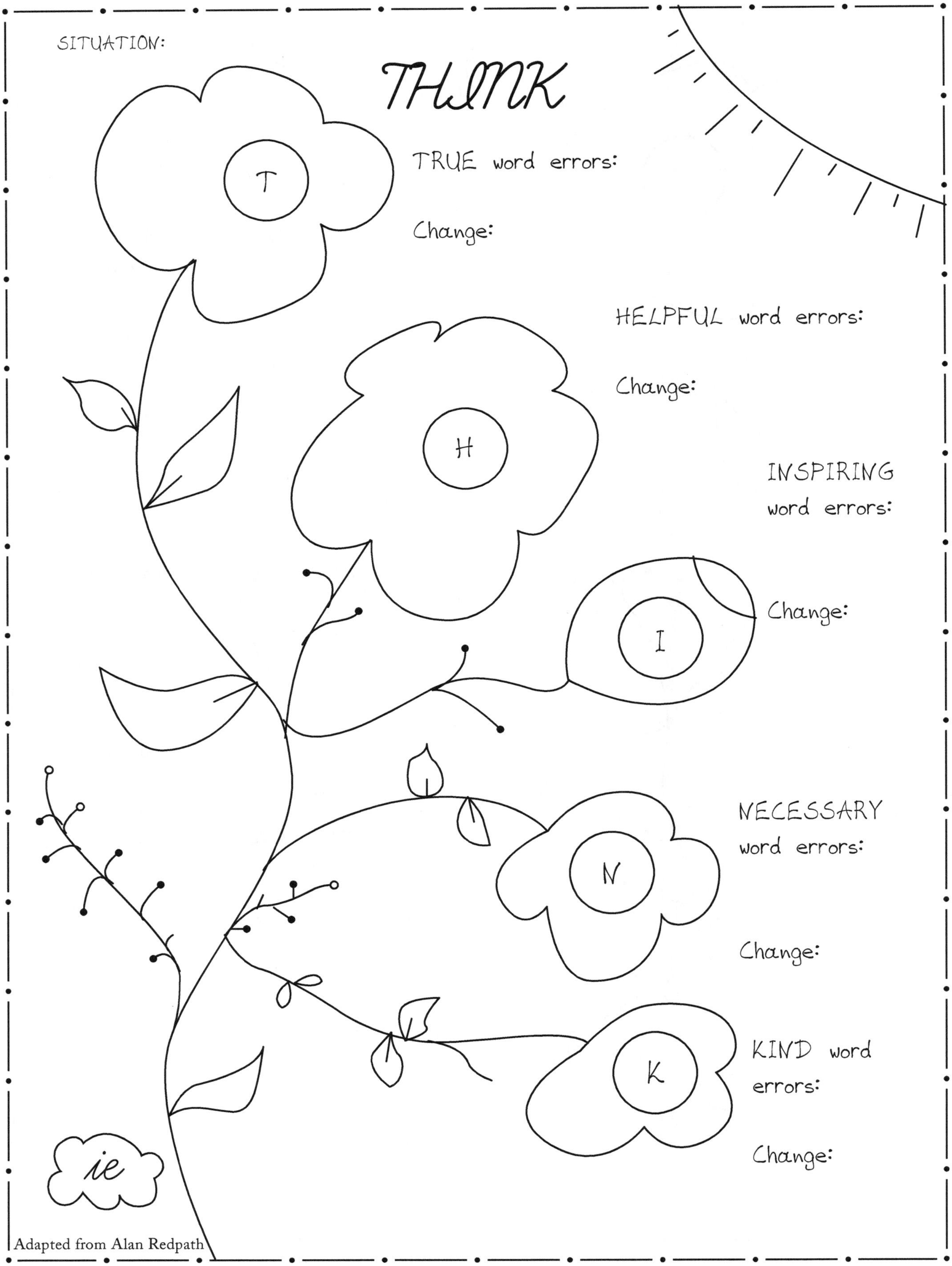
SITUATION:
THINK
T
TRUE word errors:
Change:
HELPFUL word errors:
Change:
H
INSPIRING word errors:
Change:
I
NECESSARY word errors:
N
Change:
K
KIND word errors:
Change:
ie
Adapted from Alan Redpath

5. The Four Horsemen

"The Four Horsemen" is an interpersonal effectiveness skill, discussed by Moonshine (2008), and identifies behavior that causes stress or damage to teens' relationships with others. Over time, when teens consistently engage in these behaviors, it can cause significant damage leading to the end of relationships.

Some examples of the four horsemen behaviors include: bullying, disobedience, refusing to communicate, and not accepting responsibility. It is important for teens to identify and to take responsibility for their own hurtful behaviors in order to avoid bringing or keeping them in their relationships.

Let's look at the four horsemen in more detail:

1. Judgmental attitude: Using words, tone of voice, or body language to show disapproval of another person. Judgmental attitudes come across as being overly critical of others and include: mean, sarcastic, or rude comments, name calling, mimicking, and ridiculing with words or body language (eye rolling, shoulder shrugs).

2. Disobedient behavior: Refusal to obey rules within the family, school or church, or to someone in authority. The need to reduce disobedient behavior applies to a teen even if they feel the rules are "unfair." A few examples are: skipping school or church, stealing, lying by commission or omission, and refusing to comply with any house rules.

3. Deny responsibility (of the problem): Refusing or not being open to look at your part of the problem. Some examples are: blaming, not accepting responsibility, making excuses, and refusing to apologize.

4. Shut down: When the teen physically or emotionally withdraws from the conversation or interpersonal interaction. A few examples of this behavior include: tuning the other person out, physically turning away, acting too busy, refusing to answer or make eye contact, and overuse of video games.

~ Handout Directions ~

Give a handout to each teen. Teach them the interpersonal effectiveness skill, "The Four Horsemen," and suggest how these four behaviors cause stress or damage to relationships. Also, inform the teens that if they consistently engage in four horsemen behaviors it could possibly lead to the end of the relationship.

Discuss each of the four behaviors, and provide examples to clearly illustrate them. Also, ask teens if they have been on the receiving end of any of these behaviors, and how it made them feel. Sometimes, reflecting on our own experience is the best way to develop empathy for others, and may help to curtail the teens' probability of engaging in these behaviors.

The Four Horsemen

...behaviors that end relationships

Judgmental attitude: Words, tone of voice, or body language to show disapproval of another person, for example: sarcastic or rude comments, eye rolling.

Disobedient behavior: Refusal to obey rules in school, family or church, or to someone in authority, for example: lying, stealing, skipping school.

Deny responsibility: Refusing or not being open to look at your part of the problem, for example: blaming, making excuses, refusing to apologize.

Shut down: Physically or emotionally withdrawn from conversation or interaction, for example: turning away, refusing to answer or make eye contact.

~ Worksheet Directions ~

Give a worksheet to each teen. Review The Four Horsemen, its role in the end of relationships, and examples of each of the four behaviors.

Ask the teens to identify a current or past relationship in their life. Instead of focusing on the other person, we will challenge the teens to rise to the healthiest choice, and focus on themselves. As such, teens will examine the relationship, and notice any four horsemen behaviors they have chosen in the relationship. Next, they will ponder their DBT skills, and identify DBT strategies they could have used instead of the harmful behavior.

The teens can also cope ahead and look to possible future interactions, identify four horsemen behavior and strategies to manage or eliminate those behaviors.

As a group, discuss the following vignette and completed example sheet. Prompt the teens to name additional DBT skills Millie could have used to assist her in managing her four horsemen behaviors.

Vignette

Millie is a 15-year-old sophomore. Millie has a hard time getting along and following her parents' rules. Millie thinks that their rules are "annoying and dumb."

Millie admits that she wants to have a better relationship with both her mom and dad, and her siblings too. She fills out the Four Horsemen sheet with her therapist.

The Four Horsemen ie

…behaviors that end relationships

• **Judgmental attitude:** • Behaviors I notice in me: When I get mad at my parents I roll my eyes and say rude things.

• DBT strategies: Square breathing, stay non-judgmental.

Disobedient behavior: • Behaviors I notice in me: I try to find ways around my parents' rules at home, especially curfew.

•DBT strategies: Opposite Action (plan to come home early).

Deny Responsibility: • Behaviors I notice in me: Blame my parents when I get in trouble for being late.
•DBT strategies: GIVE—be gentle with my parents; practice Radical Acceptance—"These are the rules—I'm going to accept them."

Shut down: • Behaviors I notice in me: I often turn away and refuse to listen to discussions with my parents.
•DBT strategies: Willing—open hands, and repair—I'll apologize for my choices.

The Four Horsemen ie

…behaviors that end relationships

Judgmental attitude: • Behaviors I notice in me:

• DBT strategies:

Disobedient behavior: • Behaviors I notice in me:

• DBT strategies:

Deny responsibility: • Behaviors I notice in me:

• DBT strategies:

Shut down: • Behaviors I notice in me:

• DBT strategies:

6. GIVE

GIVE is an interpersonal effectiveness skill, and offers guidelines for keeping relationships. The acronym helps teens to remember the steps of the skill:

G = Be gentle. In talking with others, stay nice and respectful. Do not: attack, threaten, judge, or use mocking facial expressions or body language.

I = Act interested. Show that you are interested in the other person while you talk with them. Show interest with your body language: eye contact, face your body towards theirs, and listen with both ears! Do not interrupt.

V = Validate. When you engage in a conversation or spend time with someone, put other distractions (phone, movies, other conversations) aside. Listen and let them know that you understand their point of view, even if it differs from yours. Use sentence starters like: "It makes sense to me that…" or "It sounds like what you're saying is…"

E = Easy manner. Remember to get along with others, be nice, and smile. There is an old saying, "You catch more flies with honey than with vinegar." Which would you prefer: honey or vinegar?

~ *Handout Directions* ~

Pass a handout to each teen. Explain the GIVE skill. Go over each letter and its meaning. Provide a vignette or life example to further review each letter.

GIVE

G =  *be gentle*

Do not:

- attack
- judge
- mock

I =  (ACT)

Interested:

- eye contact
- listen
- don't interrupt

V = *validate...*

put {ALL} distractions aside, and understand their point of view. Show this by saying:

"It makes sense to me that..."
"It sounds like what you're saying is..."

E = *easy manner*

Adapted from Linehan, *DBT Skills Training Manual* (2015b)

~ Worksheet Directions ~

Give a worksheet to each teen. Review the GIVE skill, or elicit help from a teen to review the letters and their meanings.

Ask the teens to practice the skill by using a life example, or provide vignettes for them to use. Teens will write the situation at the top-left corner of the page. Based on the situation, teens will answer each of the questions on the worksheet. The questions correspond to each letter of the skill, GIVE.

Vignette

The completed worksheet will be based on the following vignette: William is 14 years old and is a freshman at high school. He likes school and has friends, but doesn't consider himself to be in the popular group. William likes to hang out with his friends during lunch in the quadrangle. Yesterday, during lunch, William was throwing a frisbee with his long-time buddy, Paul.

Paul threw the frisbee past William's reach several times, almost hitting a number of girls in the process. After the last throw, Paul laughed and said, "That's one way to get you to talk to some girls."

William felt angry and thought, "Paul's throwing it out of my reach on purpose to embarrass me."

GIVE

ie

Situation: Paul throwing frisbee out of my reach

G *(be gentle)* Ways I can be gentle:

- open hands
- kind words
- stick to the facts, "Hey, can you throw it closer to me?"

I *(act interested)* Ways I can act interested:

- keep eye contact
- listen to his point of view

V *(validate)* Validating comments that I could say, after pulling him aside:

- "I know you're trying to help me, but I don't want the frisbee to hit anyone."

E *(easy manner)* Easy manner:

- half-smiling

Adapted from Linehan, *DBT Skills Training Manual* (2015b)

GIVE

ie

Situation:

G *(be gentle)* Ways I can be gentle:

I *(act interested)* Ways I can act interested:

V *(validate)* Validating comments that I could say:

E *(easy manner)* Easy manner:

Adapted from Linehan, *DBT Skills Training Manual* (2015b)

7. FAST

FAST is an acronym for guidelines to self-respect in relationships. Let's look further at each letter in this interpersonal effectiveness skill:

F = Be fair. Stay fair to yourself as well as the other person. Practice validation with yourself and the other individual in the situation.

A = No apologies. Apologize for your mistake or wrongdoing. Be careful not to get into a victim role and over-apologize. Apologize once with your head held high.

S = Stick to values. Stay true to who you are and your values. Do not change your values to win others' friendship or attention; in the long run it will be a disaster.

T = Be truthful. Stay in the truth; be honest. Do not make excuses or exaggerate the truth.

~ *Handout Directions* ~

Provide a handout to each teen. Teach the FAST skill, each of the letters in the acronym, and its meaning. Discuss a life situation or vignette to further illustrate each letter of the skill.

FAST

ie

F =

BE FAIR

- Be fair to yourself and to others.
- Validate your feelings and needs and those of others.

A =

APOLOGY

- Apologize for your mistake or wrongdoing.
- Don't over-apologize.
- Stay calm in your apology.

S =

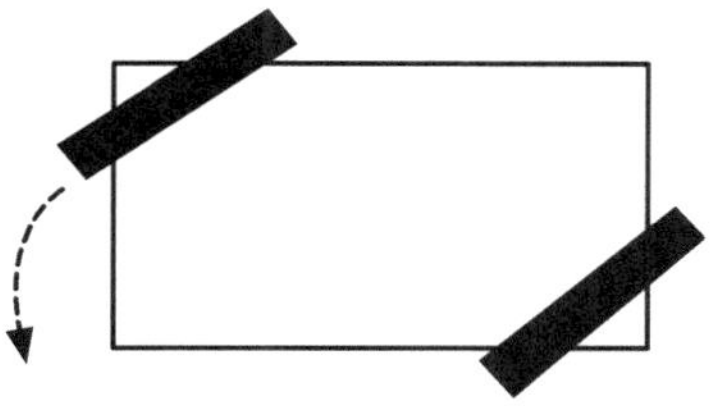

"STICK" TO YOUR VALUES

- Stay true to who you are and to your values.
- Don't abandon your beliefs for others.

T =

BE TRUTHFUL

- Stay in an honest place.
- Don't make excuses or exaggerate.

Adapted from Linehan, *DBT Skills Training Manual* (2015b)

~ Worksheet Directions ~

Give a worksheet to each teen. Review the FAST skill, or elicit help from a teen to review the letters and their meanings.

Ask the teens to practice the skill by using a life example, or provide vignettes for them to use. Teens will write the situation at the top-left corner of the page. Based on the situation, teens will answer each of the questions on the worksheet. The questions correspond to each letter of the skill, FAST.

Vignette

The vignette will be reflected in the completed worksheet. Lexi is 14 years old. She has been in dance since the age of 12. Some of the other girls at the studio are jealous of her because she's fairly new, and she's very good. As a matter of fact, she often gets parts in musicals that they wanted and tried out for.

Lately, Lexi has been noticing the other girls whispering and leaving her out of conversations and activities. During the break, she overheard the girls making plans to go to the mall together. No one invited her.

FAST

Situation: I wasn't invited to the mall. I'm being left out a lot.

F = (be fair) Ways I can be fair:

I plan to ask one of the girls why they're leaving me out. I'm going to say to myself, "It's okay to have hurt feelings."

A = (don't over-apologize) Ways and comments for apologizing:

When I talk, I'll hold my head up high.

S = (stick to my values) Validating comments as I stick to my values:

I'm going to continue in dance, and dance to the best of my ability.

T = (be truthful) Ways and comments as I am being truthful:

I plan to be nice, and say the truth— "It's hurtful to me."

Adapted from Linehan, *DBT Skills Training Manual* (2015b)

FAST

ie

Situation:

= (be fair)

Ways I can be fair:

A = (don't over-apologize)

Ways and comments for apologizing:

S = (stick to my values)

Validating comments as I stick to my values:

T = (be truthful)

Ways and comments as I am being truthful:

Adapted from Linehan, *DBT Skills Training Manual* (2015b)

References

Behavioral Tech: A Linehan Institute Training Company. Available at: www.behavioraltech.org (accessed September 20, 2017).

Linehan, M.M. (2015a) *DBT Skills Training Handouts and Worksheets*, 2nd edition. New York: The Guilford Press.

Linehan, M.M. (2015b) *DBT Skills Training Manual, 2nd edition*. New York: The Guilford Press.

Mazza, J.J., Dexter-Mazza, E.T., Miller, A.L., Rathus, J.H., and Murphy, H.E. (2016) *DBT Skills in Schools: Skills Training for Emotional Problem Solving for Adolescents (DBT STEPS-A)*. New York: The Guilford Press.

Moonshine, C. (2008) *Acquiring Competency and Achieving Proficiency with Dialectical Behavior Therapy, Volume II: The Worksheets*. Eau Claire, WI: PESI Healthcare.

Nhat Hanh, T. (2011) *Planting Seeds: Practicing Mindfulness with Children*. Berkeley, CA: Parallax Press.

Rathus, J.H. and Miller, A.L. (2015) *DBT Skills Manual for Adolescents*. New York: The Guilford Press.

Carol Lozier, MSW, LCSW, has a Bachelor of Arts degree in Psychology and Criminal Justice from Indiana University. She also received a Masters in Clinical Social Work from Florida State University in 1989. Ms. Lozier is a licensed therapist in Kentucky, and has been in private practice since 1998.

Ms. Lozier specializes in trauma, and adopted and foster children, teens, and adults. In her practice, she counsels in individual, family, and group therapy. Ms. Lozier conducts a Dialectical Behavior Therapy (DBT) skills group with preteens and teens.

Ms. Lozier has a passion to work with children, teens, and adults who have experienced any level of trauma. Within the past 15 years, she has specialized in helping adoptive and foster families in the trenches. Carol is the author of the following books: *The Adoptive & Foster Parent Guide: How to Heal Your Child's Trauma and Loss* (2012), *Devotions of Comfort and Hope for Adoptive & Foster Moms* (2013), *Clothed In Armor: Spiritual Warfare for Kids* (2015) and *Clothed in Armor: Spiritual Warfare for Adoptive & Foster Kids* (2015).